Neve Campbell

Neve Campbell

Kathleen Tracy

ECW Press

The publication of *Neve Campbell* has been generously supported by
the Government of Canada through the Book Publishing
Industry Development Program.

CANADIAN CATALOGUING IN PUBLICATION DATA

Tracy, Kathleen
Neve Campbell

ISBN 1-55022-401-8

1. Campbell, Neve. 2. Motion picture actors and actresses – Canada – Biography.
3. Television actors and actresses – Canada –Biography. I. Title.
PB2308.C35T72 2000 791.43'028'092 C00-930432-0

Back cover photo by Karen Hardy / London Features
Cover design by Guylaine Régimbald.
Interior design by Yolande Martel.
This book is set in Perpetua and Rotis SansSerif.

Printed by Printcrafters Inc., Winnipeg, Manitoba, Canada.
Distributed in Canada by General Distribution Services,
325 Humber College Blvd., Etobicoke, Ontario M9W 7C3.
Distributed in the United States by LPC Group,
1436 West Randolph Street, Chicago, Illinois, 60607. U.S.A.

Published by ECW PRESS,
2120 Queen Street East, Suite 200,
Toronto, Ontario M4E 1E2.
ecwpress.com

PRINTED AND BOUND IN CANADA

Contents

Neve
Introduction

On *Party of Five*, Neve Campbell plays the beautiful, all-American girl next door, which just goes to show what a good actress this Canadian native really is. However, despite her high-profile roles in that television series and in films such as the *Scream* trilogy, Campbell's dramatic talents may have generated less attention than her physical attributes. What's particularly ironic about Neve's ascension as a '90s Internet and teen magazine pin-up girl is that a close look at her career shows choices based more on personal taste than personal ambition, on an apparent desire to stretch as an actress as opposed to a hunger for celebrity.

Unlike many young stars of today who knew from childhood they wanted to be the next Bruce Willis or Meryl Streep, Campbell grew up wanting to be a dancer, but had to give up that dream while still a child when the unique pressures of dance forced her out. Because of that, Neve seems to view her acting success through wary eyes. Even though she has worked almost nonstop for the past several years, she seems to take little pleasure from her success and has exuded at times a curious "this too probably shall pass" resignation. While peers such as Sarah Michelle Gellar and Claire Danes are comfortable and confident with their evolution from television actress to touted film star of tomorrow, Campbell — whose movies have solidly done better box office than those of either Gellar or Danes — seems hesitant to acknowledge her place as one of Hollywood's bright stars of the new millennium, as if to do so would be either unseemly or a jinx.

Regardless of her public face, as far as the movie world's power brokers are concerned, Campbell is a leading lady to be reckoned with and will remain a sought-after property for many years to come. But having already once buckled emotionally under the pressure of having to meet high levels of expectation while a young dancer, Campbell knows better than most the importance of learning to cope with the unrelenting interest of fans and press alike — the personal scrutiny and attention that is the true, ultimate price of success in the age of new media.

1 A Singular Childhood

Neve

When most Americans think of Canada, virgin landscapes, a pristine natural environment of snow-capped mountains, and lush forests filled with thriving flora and fauna are the first images to greet the mind's eye. And while Canada's natural resources are indeed the envy of many a nation, America's northern neighbor also has a more urban, less romantic reality that can be found in its share of industrial regions. While the urban blight that has rotted many of America's troubled inner cities may not yet be part of the Canadian lexicon, middle-class families juggling to get by financially are just as much a part of the national makeup as they are in any other industrialized country. So in that regard, Neve Campbell's upbringing was unremarkably similar to that of millions of others. At the same time, she lived a singular childhood.

Campbell was born in the city of Guelph in the province of Ontario, about an hour outside of Toronto. Today, Guelph is a vibrant community of over 100,000 people located in the heart of what is called Canada's Technology Triangle. But behind its modern profile, Guelph has a rich history. It was founded on St. George's Day in 1827 and is distinguished as being one of the first planned towns in Canada. The location of the city was chosen by a then well-known Scottish novelist named John Galt, whose intention was to attract settlers to the area by designing an aesthetically pleasing city. The result was European-flavored, with the plaza-filled town radiating outward from the Speed River. Galt dubbed the city Guelph after one of the family names of the British royal family, hence Guelph's enduring nickname, the Royal City.

But it was a case of the best-laid plans not living up to the high expectations behind them. Despite Galt's vision, Guelph didn't become the metropolitan hub he had hoped it would. It remained a quaint village, with a substantial Scottish community, until 1856 when the Grand Trunk Railroad finally connected it to Toronto. By the time Neve Campbell was born on October 3, 1973, Guelph was a full-fledged city, close enough to its burgeoning neighbor to reap the benefits of Toronto's evolution into an ever more important international presence, but far enough away from Toronto to retain its own charm. Neve appreciated growing up within the Scottish community, which allowed her to "experience a lot of traditional Scottish things," such as the food haggis — Campbell says it "tastes great."

But it was more her personal surroundings that would steer Neve's course in life. Considering the family she was born into, it seems almost predetermined that Neve, as well as her older brother Christian, would grow up to be a performer of some kind. First, there was the unique name. Neve was her mother's maiden name, and although in the Dutch of her native Amsterdam it was pronounced *nayfa*, the Campbells gave their daughter the anglicized pronunciation of *nev*. Then there was the family legacy. Her father, Gerry, who was of Scottish descent, was a high-school drama teacher and her Dutch mother, Marnie, ran a dinner theater that presented murder mysteries. In fact, her parents met while performing in a play together.

"We didn't really have a choice," Neve says of performing, to Sherry Weiner of *UniverCity*. "My father teaches drama in high school and directs an amateur Scottish theater group and my mother owned a dinner theater, so I was surrounded by it. My grandparents on my father's side used to perform for soldiers during the war and on my mother's side had a theater company in Holland. When my brother and I were two and one, we have a picture of him carrying me around in my diapers dancing in the living room."

Her brother Christian holds that photo just as dear. "That's the way I was raised," he told Jodi Bryson of *Sassy* magazine. "Our lives were centered around performing."

But in addition to performing, another legacy was passed down to Neve. "My mother says that on the day I was born," Campbell recalls, "she looked in my eyes and said I was one day old going on thirty. I guess I'm what is called an old soul."

Either that, or Neve's sensitive nature, even as an infant, had picked up on the tension rife in her household. When she was still a baby, Neve's parents divorced and both subsequently remarried, with Neve's dad getting custody of her and Christian. The separation from her mom, who she saw only every other weekend, left a permanent emotional mark on Neve. Although she loved her dad, she points out, "You can't talk about everything with your father. There are certain things you can relate only to your mother."

That said, despite their animosity toward each other, Neve was able to learn lessons from both her parents. "From my dad, I learned how to appreciate what you have in life," she told Geri Richter Campbell of *Jane* magazine. "And how to drywall and how to make chicken curry, and to appreciate running in the rain. Whenever it would pour in Toronto, my dad would take off his shirt and go running down the street in the rain." From her mother, Neve says she gleaned "spirituality, and to be nonjudgmental toward others. She taught me how to do yoga, and if you have any difficulties in life, remember to breathe."

Adding extended family in heaps, both Gerry and Marnie divorced their respective spouses, with Gerry later remarrying yet again. Keeping familial cohesiveness when under one roof is hard enough, but Campbell's fractured domestic life left Neve, the child, anchorless, especially since her parents weren't on particularly amicable terms. "It wasn't a horrible situation, but you're forced to grow up a little more quickly. It's something that impacted my life from an early age. When you don't have a solid family grounding," she says pointedly, "you have to take care of yourself."

When she was six years old, Neve experienced a life-turning moment when Gerry took her to see a performance of *The Nutcracker*. After watching, mesmerized, Neve emerged from the theater knowing what she wanted more than anything: "Becoming a ballet dancer became my dream."

It doesn't take a psychiatry degree to understand that a desire to control her environment and find a constant in life is what lay behind Neve's yearning to dance, a desire that emerged when she was still a child of six, which is when she began training in earnest. Plus, through dance, Neve could express emotions otherwise held in check.

"I think as a child, I held a lot of stuff," Campbell tells *Rough Cut*'s Veronica Mixon. "So, if there was anger, it was held in because it wasn't allowed to come out. My father's from lower-class Glasgow and my grandparents went through very difficult times during the war. They had a lot of struggles, and it wasn't really okay to complain."

Not only was complaining frowned upon, any kind of demonstrative emotion was discouraged — although Neve wasn't always successful in keeping her feelings completely under wraps. "You always knew when she was pissed off," remembers Christian. "This sullen darkness would come over her face. She wouldn't complain, but you knew she was upset." But more often than not, Neve would swallow those feelings. As she told Louis B. Hobson of the *London Free Press*, "We were not encouraged to express our emotions. It was considered bad manners. I escaped through dance."

Campbell believes that is why "I love acting and why I love dance, because I didn't really feel free to express my emotions as a child. So getting up on a stage and doing it through physical activity was an outlet for me."

But at first glance, Neve didn't seem a likely candidate for the fairy-princess world of ballerinas. "I was geeky," she admits to *Australian TV Week*. "I was skinny and had huge feet and knobby knees. I grew up with three brothers and my dad, so girlie things were never my thing. My style was what my dad threw me in — corduroys and a shirt, and I mucked them up a lot."

Campbell also admits to being less than neat. "As a child, I was an untidy person. My brother used to come into my room and it bothered him so much he would clean it up and decorate it, because it was such a mess."

The multitalented Neve in *Catwalk*

EVERETT COLLECTION

Sloppiness and tomboyishness notwithstanding, Gerry Campbell picked up on his daughter's dream and made it into one of his own, seeing his daughter as the performer he had never been. "He was very wonderful in that he really pushed me in this business," Neve notes. "He pushed my brother also. Both my parents were actors and got married at such a young age and had us at such young ages and didn't get to finish their careers.

"My father really believed in my brother and me. Sometimes it was hard, because he pushed us when we wanted to quit — but that's okay, because I wouldn't be where I am now."

Although Neve was encouraged by her family to pursue her desire to dance, her peers at school offered little if any support. "I was pretty much a loser. I had absolutely no friends," she says. Campbell recalls not only being far outside the in crowd, but also outright unpopular, citing a particularly painful Valentine's Day as exhibit A: "We had this awful thing at school where we had cookies on Valentine's Day, and every student could buy them and send them to other class members," Campbell tells *TV Guide*.

Popular students wore a trail in the floor between their desks and the front of the room, while Neve sat and watched the parade. "They would call up each student every time their name came out of the box. I wasn't called up. Wait, I was called up *once* because the teacher gave me a cookie. I was devastated. No one would spend five cents to send me a cookie."

Looking back as an adult, Campbell realizes she shares part of the responsibility for being such an outsider. "I couldn't relate to kids when I was young," she admits. "I don't know — jokes just to be giddy didn't make a lot of sense to me. I think I had grown up fairly quickly in my childhood, probably because of family circumstances. Also, because I was so focused on dancing and other things in life, I didn't relate to the childhood mentality. So my childhood was basically nil."

Even on those occasions where she was involved with the group, the results were usually disappointing, such as her first kiss with a classmate named Larry. "I was, like, six years old, and we were having a kissing contest in school, to see who could kiss the longest," Neve recalls in a *Cosmopolitan* interview with Jancee Dunn.

However, the boy who Neve really had her eyes on was Sammy Williamson. "I totally had a big crush on him. I remember us kicking and hitting each other a lot — which is, of course, the way you flirt when you're a kid. He kinda had a crush on me too, but he also liked another girl called Andrea, and I wasn't very happy about that. When we had this kissing contest I wanted to kiss Sammy, but he was doing it with Andrea so I had to kiss Larry. . . . It was at recess and it was meant to be who could kiss the longest. I kissed Larry and it only lasted about three seconds. I thought I was going to throw up afterwards, because he'd just eaten a peanut butter sandwich and it was all over the inside of his mouth."

And, she tells Dunn, Larry "had the worst breath on earth. And I was mad at him the rest of the day because we lost."

That sensation of being adrift from her peers made the world of fantasy that much more appealing to Neve. Every Wednesday night, she and her father would go to a movie house that screened classic cinema. "We'd see foreign films, old black-and-white films," Neve recalls fondly. "I think I grew up liking films that took a lot of time. The humor or moral of the story wasn't just shoved in your face."

And, more than anywhere else, Neve found emotional solace in dance, where the only thing that mattered was hard work and accomplishment. And where being onstage meant being able to be someone else, even if just for a moment. "I remember when I realized how important it was for her to be onstage," says her brother Christian. He recalls the time he was ten years old and their father was directing a high-school production of *H.M.S. Pinafore*. Gerry had created a role so that Christian could be in the production, but hadn't done the same for Neve. "I came into the living room all dressed up in my little costume," Christian says, "and Neve broke into tears because she felt so left out."

When she was nine, Neve auditioned to attend the prestigious — and extremely competitive — National Ballet School of Canada, located in Toronto. Considered one of the leading schools in the world, it is touted, according its own literature, "for providing the best in ballet training integrated with an enriched academic program, plus residences all on one site. . . . From the some 1,000 young dancers who audition each year, approximately 45 are accepted into the full-time Professional Ballet/Academic Program which accommodates 150 students from across Canada and around the world in grades 5 through 12. . . . If dance is your dream, NBS is your school."

Dance was Neve's only dream, so, along with dozens of other aspiring ballerinas, Neve danced her dance then anxiously waited to hear whether or not she would be accepted. Making the wait particularly nerve-wracking was the added fact that Neve desperately had to go to the bathroom. "When the principal called me into her office to tell me that I was accepted, I had to pee so badly, I had to hold myself!" she laughs.

The importance of her acceptance to the school wasn't lost on Neve. "I wanted to be there because I wanted to be a dancer. I love to dance, and that was my dream. When you're in that school, it means you've beaten out two thousand people to get there," she tells Jane Wollman Rusoff during a *Mr. Showbiz* interview. But attending the National Ballet School also meant Campbell would have to leave her hometown to live in residence and be even more removed from her already disjointed family.

If Neve had thought that being surrounded by other youths who shared her passion for dance would suddenly make her less of an outsider, she learned quickly that, if anything, being in such a competitive environment heightened the stakes and sharpened the barbs.

"I had no friends, I didn't fit in, and I was living in residence. When you live with the people you don't fit in with, you're in trouble," she says. "I was definitely the loser of my class. They even had a song about me, and how ugly I was. It described each girl in my class, from the prettiest to the ugliest, and I was the last one. The end of the song just went, '*Neve-urrggh, Neve-urrggh*,' like they were throwing up. Beautiful! I was very flattered," she says dryly. "I used to go home and cry."

Her name was also the butt of schoolboy humor. "I'd get 'Nevster' and 'Campbell Soup makes you poop.' I'd be like, 'Ho ho ho — I've never heard that before.'"

But it wasn't just her name or physical attributes that were at the crux of the taunting. "When you're a kid and you don't fit in, then you're going to get called ugly no matter what. And I didn't fit in." As a result, Neve says, "I was always in need, in need of love, in need of my family and friends — in need of being accepted. I would try, like any kid, desperately every moment, thinking, 'Oh, they smiled at me. Wait, maybe they do like me!'"

Like many alienated youngsters, Campbell sought out entertainment to fill some of the void within. "You know who I really used to like?" she asks. "The Wonder Twins! They were awesome! They were always together and their power's together. Superheroes are very powerful, but it could make for a lonely life."

So could living under the stress of competition on a daily basis. "I can't say that I hated the school," Neve tells Jane Wollman Rusoff, "but the pressure — we were all competing for the same goal: to get into the National Ballet of Canada. It's the best dance school in the world, but an extremely competitive one, and there was a lot of pressure for a child. It had an extremely back-stabbing mentality, and there was a lot of favoritism."

Neve believes that her modest family background also contributed to her low status at the school, among children who came from much wealthier and more well-heeled homes. Then, of course, Neve didn't always help her own cause with some of her fashion statements.

"When I was 13, I decided to go to Little Italy in Toronto and have my hair permed," she recalls. "I ended up looking like Bozo the Clown. I had like really tight ringlets and I sat crying for about four hours with my mom saying, 'You look great!' All the while she was taking pictures of me. It was horrifying!"

Another time, in the early 1980s, Neve decided to rebel against her snobby schoolmates by going punk. "As much of a punk as I could be while going to a ballet school! There was a rule that our hair had to be lower than our shoulder blades and we had to wear it up in a bun. One month I was really upset with the school and I went and had the back of my head shaved, so that when I had my hair up, the bun sat on the back of a bald head. They were not happy with me at all. I would've been kicked out for anything more than that. All I could get away with was that incident and wearing my dad's university leather jacket. That was my rebellion."

But the mischievous pleasure Neve derived from such expressions of individuality was short-lived because every day the unrelenting pressure to perform weighed on her, turning her school experience into job-related drudgery. "The school was about discipline," Neve says. "We practised three to five hours a day." And students were not allowed to rest on their laurels. "Every year," recalls Campbell to the *Toronto Sun*'s Bob Thompson, "they send you a letter letting you know if you can stay."

While at the school, Neve's abilities progressed and she appeared onstage in productions of *Sleeping Beauty* and *The Nutcracker*. "I worked so hard and I truly love to dance — it's my passion." But even for children in the prime of youth, dance can be physically exhausting, and Neve developed injuries that will follow her throughout her life. "I have arthritis already, hip problems," Campbell tells *JournalNow* reporter Roger Moore.

But more than the physical toll, it was the toll the fishbowl pressure was taking on her psyche that finally made Neve scream Uncle! "I got to a place at school where I hated dance because of all the pressure, and that was really tragic for me," she says. "It was a horrible atmosphere where one's self-worth was beaten into submission. I had no friends and I didn't fit in and was very unhappy."

Many of her conflicting emotions about the school stemmed from the contradiction between what the school had to offer professionally and the cost it could exact. "The best dancers in the world come out of there — and the most messed-up people sometimes come out of there," she tells Jamie Portman of the *Ottawa Citizen*. "I mean, they're wonderful and try to take care of you, but they have many, many psychologists on staff, so that kind of tells you something about it."

Campbell tells *Rough Cut*'s Veronica Mixon solemnly, "I was fourteen, and from fifth to thirteenth grade, all you ever aspire to do is get into the company." Because of that, Neve points out, "You're not exactly going to quit. But I did, at fourteen. I was working so much during school that I wasn't happy. I wouldn't have been able to function had I stayed there. It was a huge decision. But I'd just about given up on my dream of being a dancer and realized that I couldn't have continued if I'd stayed there." Plus, Campbell says, she "didn't want to hate dancing."

Neve describes her emotional state at the time as being clinical. "Basically, I had a nervous breakdown." However, she's reluctant to dredge up too many specifics about a devastating period in her life. "I don't want to go into too much detail about it because nervous breakdowns don't necessarily mean that you hole up in a therapist's office for a month," she tells Jancee Dunn. "It was just a huge transition in my life where there was too much pressure going on."

Desperate to find some normalcy in her life, hoping it would help ease the pain of the abandonment of her childhood dream, Neve sought to immerse herself in a more traditional high school experience. But she decided to do it on her own. Instead of moving back into the family home, Neve moved in with her brother Christian and enrolled in the tenth grade at Toronto's Claude Watson School for the Arts, an alternative program that offers flexible schedules for artists, actors, and athletes — even though she already thought her performing days were behind her.

"When I quit, I thought I would never dance again," Neve muses. But that changed after a chance meeting with some other dancers, who encouraged Campbell to audition for the upcoming Toronto production of *Phantom of the Opera*, directed by Broadway legend Hal Prince. After continued prompting, Neve put her dancing shoes back on. "It was the first big Broadway production in Canada in a long time, a very big deal. I just went along for the experience. There were like three hundred girls at this cattle-call audition and I was so nervous that, when they called me, I ran off to the dressing room, I was bawling my eyes out," Campbell recalls.

Paralyzed by fear, Neve was ready to bail on the audition, until the other dancers convinced her to see it through. It was then that Neve got some much-needed comic relief. "When they called my name for the next twelve girls to go into the cattle call, they said, *Nevay Camembera*," she tells *Listen Up* reporter Craig Modderno, laughing. "All of a sudden I was a cheese. Now, how they got that, I have no idea."

With her tension subsiding, Neve auditioned. And auditioned. And auditioned. "And they kept calling me in again and again all day long," continues Neve. "Everyone got cut but eight of us. I ended up in the ballet chorus." In 1990, at only fifteen years old, Campbell became the youngest dancer ever to appear in the *Phantom* corps de ballet. The next-youngest dancer in her cast was twenty-four, nine years older.

Eventually, Campbell was given the role of the Degas Girl and ended up staying with the original Toronto cast for two years, performing over eight hundred shows. "I was one of the highest-paid professional dancers in Canada, making as much as the stars of the National Ballet," Neve says proudly. What gave Campbell particular pleasure was that despite being forced out of school, thanks to the intolerable atmosphere, she ended up "performing with dancers from the National Ballet of Canada after all. Funny how things work out," she tells *Sassy*'s Jodi Bryson.

Now a working professional, Neve decided to drop out of school completely. "I've been training since I was six, and all of a sudden I'm fifteen and the member of a fantastic company. So it didn't make a lot of sense to say, 'Oh, I'm not going to take *The Phantom of the Opera* because I need to learn more about history.'"

The two years Neve spent with *Phantom* went a great way toward helping make up for the years of torment she had suffered at the National Ballet school. "I still think of that as the best experience of my life," Campbell tells Bernard Weintraub in an interview in *Cosmopolitan*. "I was so young and extremely enthusiastic. Everyone in the cast was older and they all looked after me and showed me the ropes. I loved it!"

Leaving dance for a while allowed Campbell to find "a healthier place in my life." Ironically, though, it also made clear to Neve that her future did not lie in dance. Campbell tells Roger Moore, "I couldn't relate to the dance mentality. I cannot relate to not eating, to the back-stabbing, to doing something that will keep you in pain. You could be in the corps de ballet the entire time, know the same thirty people for the rest of your career."

With a heightened sense of self-awareness and accomplishment, Campbell was able to look to the future with hope instead of the trepidation she had suffered just a few years earlier.

"When I look back on it now," she tells Christy Slewinski of the *New York Daily News*, "I'm so glad that the one thing that I had in my life was my belief that everything in life is a learning experience, whether it be positive or negative. If you can see it as a learning experience, you can turn any negative into a positive."

For Neve, the good stuff was only just beginning.

2

Neve

Testing the Waters

Even if Campbell had wanted to, she might not have been in any physical shape to continue dancing much longer. In addition to chronic bunions and dancer's feet — a polite way of saying ugly feet, about which Neve gripes, "I can't find shoes because I have huge bunions from dancing!" — she also suffered from a potentially more serious hip condition.

"The dance world is very masochistic," Campbell tells *Jane*'s Geri Richter Campbell. "You see this incredible beauty and grace on the stage, and then backstage you see the pain. I had absolutely no joint left, because my bones had rubbed holes into each other. The doctor told me it was one of the worst cases he's ever seen. I have pictures at home."

So when a theatrical agent approached Neve one night after a *Phantom* performance and asked, "Do you want to try modeling?" Campbell signed up, but her dabble in modeling would prove less successful than she hoped. Although of average height for an actress at five-foot-five, Campbell is on the short side for today's modeling requirements. "I was a model for about two months. I did an ad for Sony and a lot of catalogue stuff. You know, where you have to point in a silly way at the camera. I couldn't stand modeling," Neve admits, calling it "too shallow. I think because I'd been training since I was six as a dancer and performing since I was a kid, the idea of just standing in front of a camera and not utilizing any of my talents didn't make any sense. Man, it was so horrible. All I wanted to do was make goofy faces at the photographer."

Nor did her wardrobe endear Neve to the profession. "I did something for Avon with this tacky purse. And I had to do like bra and underwear stuff, which was just devastating! I think that was my last job, then I was like, 'I'm out of here!' It didn't make sense to be just standing in front of a camera with everything being based on my looks."

Even though modeling had been a bust, Neve still had acting to fall back on. She'd never been formally trained as an actress, but she felt comfortable with the prospect of assuming a role that didn't involve dancing. In fact, perhaps deep down inside, she had always known acting was where her path lay. She tells Sherry Weiner of *UniverCity*, "My main ambition was always to be a dancer. But, as a young girl, when my father would ask me what kind of car I would be driving, I always said a limousine. And when he asked me how much money I would be making, I always said a lot of money. None of this fits with the dance world at all . . . dancers are poor . . . so, somewhere I knew."

It is ironic that despite being a drama teacher and theater director, Neve's father had never instructed his children. However, Campbell says she still learned "a great deal. But he never actually taught my older brother, Christian, and me how to act," she tells Jane Wollman Rusoff. "It was just sort of observing and watching him, and growing up in the amateur theater group in Toronto that we performed with when we were kids, which my father directed. It was really just observing the direction he gave to other people."

When Campbell finally left the security of her eight-shows-a-week schedule with *Phantom of the Opera* in 1992, the musical was on its way to becoming one of Toronto's longest-running shows and wouldn't close at the prestigious Pantages Theatre until November 1999, after 4,226 performances. Suddenly finding herself without a designated place to go when she woke up, Neve began testing the waters by auditioning for commercials and almost immediately found work. Her first commercial was for a local shopping megamall called the Eaton Centre.

"It was a silly little commercial and I only had one line," she laughs. "I'm with my two little brothers and we're having a hard time trying to decide what to buy our mother for Christmas and I say, 'Hey, guys — look what I got Mom.' And it's a pair of gloves."

Campbell also had the dubious honor of appearing in a Tampax commercial, which paid good money even if it did cause Neve the teeniest bit of bemusement. "Tampon adverts are the worst, aren't they?" she asks. "They're so unrealistic — like women are going to do all this athletic stuff wearing skintight white pants! It's ridiculous! My commercial was a gang of silly teenage girls running around school on photo day — you know, when everyone gets their picture taken for the yearbook. They're in this lineup waiting to have their pictures taken and I look in my purse to pull out a hairbrush and my tampons are in there. I look very proud of them."

In 1992, when she was still a teenager, Campbell was cast in her first major role, in the short-lived Canadian television series *Catwalk*. The series followed the trials and tribulations of six young adults who form a rock band called — what else? — Catwalk. Campbell played Daisy, a singer and, appropriately enough, dance teacher. Neve explains her character: "Daisy was an orphan, of course, and a bit of a wild one in the band that the show was centered on. I wore the most ridiculous clothing. I look at it now and go, 'Wow, times have really changed!' I had like painted leotards and then a little vest over it and my hair pooped right out and tacky earrings. It looks horrible now, and unfortunately they're still playing those same twenty-four episodes in Canada. It's got a cult following that I just can't understand."

In 1994, *Catwalk* enjoyed a run on MTV, where it also garnered a cult following. However, despite its alternative appeal, Campbell only stayed with the series for a year because of changes the writers had made, transforming Daisy from a sweet innocent into "a sex symbol sleeping with everyone in the band."

Being a Big House pin-up girl was a surreal experience for Campbell. Suddenly, she laughingly told *Australian Who* in 1996, "All my fan mail was from prisoners. I'd get some normal ones where they'd tell me they loved the show and that they watched it

The cast of *Catwalk*

EVERETT COLLECTION

all the time, and I'm like, 'Yeah, right — you're really thinking about the talent on the show.' And then I got some weird ones, like a guy who described my mouth and then every part of my body in graphic detail. All I could think was, 'Umm, when do you get out?'"

All of those state-mandated shut-ins would likely have been crushed to learn that despite her tender age, Neve was already seriously involved. Although she had been the butt of jokes among her ballet-school peer group, once she ventured out into the world, Neve discovered that many men considered her attractive and desirable. However, her lack of dating experience occasionally showed. First, she admits, "I was a tomboy and when I was a teenager I didn't wear dresses at all." Then there was the struggle to learn those all-important dating tips.

"I ordered French onion soup in a restaurant on the first official date I ever went on and it was a disaster. I thought, 'I'm just going to be dainty and order the soup.' I'd never had French onion soup before and I didn't realize that it was going to be impossible to eat. I thought it'd be a really classy thing to order. I tried desperately hard to pretend I was cool with it, but my date was just staring at me, like, 'What's the matter with you?' And of course, French onion soup isn't great for your breath. I have no idea what I was thinking."

Campbell also had a very brief nipped-in-the-bud romance with "a guy called Aaron when I was about seventeen because he used to have a mohawk. I thought he was the coolest guy. But he left me after three weeks."

Neve's dating days were mercifully short-lived. Just after she had joined *Phantom*, Campbell met Jeff Colt at a theater party. Colt was an aspiring actor who worked as a bartender at the Pantages Theatre, which housed the production. Neve and Jeff hit it off and soon were seeing a lot of each other. When she was just seventeen, the relationship had progressed to the point where Campbell moved in with Colt. But unlike other teenage girls, Neve did so with few stars in her eyes. She was skeptical about marriage and often professed doubts that she would ever exchange vows herself, having seen by her parents' example how badly nuptials could turn out.

Even though his own career had yet to take off, Colt was supportive of Neve as she went from *Catwalk* to guest-starring in Canadian-produced series such as *Kids in the Hall*, *Are You Afraid of the Dark?*, and *My Secret Identity*. (In a nifty bit of real-life foreshadowing, *My Secret Identity* co-starred a former child actor named Jerry O'Connell, who would later play Neve's boyfriend in *Scream 2*.)

Neve also made herself available for more offbeat, independent projects, such as *The Passion of John Ruskin*, a fourteen-minute short, the National Film Board of Canada-sponsored movie *Paint Cans*, and a horror film, *The Dark*, about a mutant rat. Then came the role that would ultimately lead her to Hollywood, the NBC tragedy of the week *I Know My Son Is Alive*. The telefilm, which was shot in Canada, starred Corbin Bernsen and Amanda Pays as the parents of a child who goes missing. The movie itself was eminently forgettable, but Neve wasn't. Executives at NBC, always on the lookout for fresh talent, talked Campbell into flying to Los Angeles to get a feel for the industry there, believing she had a very sellable look. Although not blonde-bombshell-cosmetically-perfect beautiful, Neve had a wholesome, natural beauty. Even her imperfections, such as the scar in the middle of her forehead, a remnant of a childhood bicycle accident, added to, rather than subtracted from, her appeal.

Hollywood welcomed Campbell with open offices, and, to her utter amazement, Neve found a manager within a week. She was also introduced to the Hollywood celebrity scene, albeit of a has-been sort. "In the first week I was in Los Angeles, I met Scott Baio," Campbell recalls. "He was trying to pick me up and told me not to bother trying to be an actress because I'd only end up on the casting couch. He was a little persistent, but I beat him at pool and I think he was a little put off by that." Neve admits that she had spent many hours in Toronto playing pool and used her expertise against the unsuspecting Baio. "I used to play all the time in Toronto. I've been known to be a shark. Mind you, I'm terrible at breaking. But I love it because it's like dancing — if you're doing it right and you have the proper technique, then you'll succeed."

That philosophy applied not only to pool and dancing, but to acting as well. A week after signing with her manager, Neve was sent out on an audition for a pilot being filmed for the Fox network, *Party of Five*, about five siblings who are left to fend for each other after their parents are killed in a car accident. What initially interested her most was the script's pedigree. "I used to watch *The Wonder Years* all the time. I loved that show," Neve says. "I just think it was an incredibly written show and the quality is really wonderful. And when I originally read the script of *Party of Five*, my manager told me it was the same producer as the one who wrote *Wonder Years*, Ken Topolsky, and that's what made me so enthusiastic about the show."

The role Neve read for was the fifteen-year-old sister, Julia. "It was a great experience, a very positive experience," Neve says of the audition process. "When I went in for the first audition, they seemed very certain right away and kind of let me know that. Then I did a couple of auditions. What I've been told is when I walked into the room, they were very happy because they'd already auditioned three hundred girls and hadn't found Julia. I read to them for two minutes, and within two weeks I was offered a role. It was very quick, very quick. I was lucky."

Everything was happening so fast, Neve needed to take a moment and weigh what it would mean to accept the job. It was one thing to leave home to attend school less than an hour away, but quite another to move thousands of miles away for a new career. It wasn't so much that Campbell was worried about being on her own — "I was already living independently on my own since I was fifteen so I wasn't scared, maybe apprehensive" — the biggest consideration was more personal. If she accepted the role in *Party of Five*, it meant leaving behind Jeff, whose entry into the United States would be subject to immigration rules and regulations.

But Neve knew how important a career move it was to accept the job in Los Angeles. "Coming from Canada, you have to move to L.A. to become successful in films because there's not enough lead roles for us in Canada." Plus, if she came down to join the cast of a series, it would be an opportunity to obtain her green card. "I only took the role as a means to get my green card," Campbell once claimed, before admitting that getting the card wasn't as simple as she had thought it would be. "It took me four years to get it and cost me $50,000 in attorney's fees, and the really crazy thing is that they were denying me the green card even while I was paying $500,000 a year in taxes," she said in exasperation. "It wasn't fair."

Welcome to America.

After returning to Canada to get her things in order, she arrived again in L.A. and tried to adjust to her new environs. The first thing she noticed was that Canadians and Americans differed in some specific ways. "We're constantly apologizing," she says of her fellow Canadians. "We're almost overly polite, which is a good thing and a bad thing. We tend to sit back, instead of being as aggressive as Americans." The second thing she realized was that she needed to tone down her sarcasm. "When I first came to L.A.," Campbell tells the *Toronto Sun*'s Bob Thompson, "I had to change my very cynical and sarcastic humor. I put a few girls in tears, because they didn't understand."

Neve's brother Christian offers that some of his sister's sharp wit was merely a smokescreen acting as armor. "It's difficult for people to tell how insecure she is, because she gives off this 'It's all right, I'm confident with myself' kind of thing. She holds all her real emotions in. That's her strength — but it's also her weakness. It makes her sort of hard to get to."

For the most part in those early days, Campbell kept to herself, finding companionship with her shih tzu, Buster, and by reading books such as Kahlil Gibran's *The Prophet*. "There's one passage about relationships," she tells Christopher John Farley of *Time*, "about two trees growing, and if they grow too close together they'll shade one another and won't be allowed to grow, but if they grow enough of a distance apart, they'll be able to grow and continue their love. I find that to be really beautiful."

No university degree is needed to appreciate the significance of that passage to Neve. She was still struggling with mixed emotions over Jeff, who wanted to join her in Los Angeles. It wasn't that she didn't love him, it was just that she was leery of getting *too* involved, because she had no interest in getting married. What did intrigue her was the fantasy of marrying her acting with her dance. "I was born in the wrong generation," she once noted. "I should have been born when Gene Kelly, Fred Astaire, and Ginger Rogers were making movies — that's when I was supposed to be a movie star."

But in the spring of 1994, Neve's first order of business was making the *Party of Five* pilot for Fox. Of all the networks then in existence, Fox seemed the least likely to be interested in a family drama, much less have the audience demographic to support it. But still the renegade network gave the go-ahead, first for the pilot, then for the pilot to become a series.

If Neve was to have handpicked a project that seemed likely to be short-lived, this was it. But then a funny thing happened after the show's September debut — television critics christened it the second coming of family drama. Ken Tucker of *Entertainment Weekly* said it was "surprisingly affecting, and, following *Melrose Place*, could well find an audience."

Marvin Kitman of *Newsday* sounded shell-shocked. "I can't believe I'm writing this, but there is a good family show on Fox, the renegade kiddie porn network. It's not silly, salacious or any of those other things on Fox that make you squirm. . . . At any rate, the network that brought prime time family to new lows with *Married . . . With Children* is making amends, atoning for its sins, by bringing you *Party of Five*, a socially responsible, heartwarming, beautifully made, written and acted series. It's the best dysfunctional family show of the year."

Matt Roush, USA *Today* television critic, compared *Party of Five* with the ultimately short-lived ABC series *On Our Own*, also about a group of orphaned children. "Imagine the odds that, over two nights of prime time, two different networks would try to sell us on separate sets of telegenic orphans, the parents lost in car accidents, each family boasting its own drooling bulldog for comic relief. Imagine the shock that, of the two, Fox has come up with the

The cast of *Catwalk*

EVERETT COLLECTION

classiest winner. *Party of Five* is the best, warmest, most immediately satisfying contemporary family drama since ABC's *Life Goes On*. May this one have as long a run. Being too good for Fox is often a death sentence. Let us pray."

Jeff Graham of *TV Guide* commented, "If you love *90210*. If you loved *Life Goes On*. If you're at all inclined to fall for a new TV family of considerable charm and four-handkerchief heart, by all means crash Fox's *Party of Five*. Simply put, it's the most likable show about orphans ever. Sorry, Annie. Sexy and cuddly, this is *Oliver* with a hipper twist. Is it too good for Fox? That could be the ultimate *Party* pooper."

People's David Hiltbrand was one of the few who seemed unimpressed, giving it a mediocre C+. "Here's hoping the Salingers misbehave. It's perverse to put together a high-gloss young cast and then saddle them with enormous responsibilities. It's like hiring the Rockettes and dressing them in space-age-like hazmat suits: It doesn't play to their strengths."

For Neve, joining *Party of Five* was another whirlwind experience. One moment she's playing fourth bananas in cheesy telefilms, the next she's squired in front of national American television critics to talk about a show she only just started working on and besieged by photographers who sense *Party of Five*'s young cast could be the Next Big Things. Typically, Campbell sought to keep perspective.

"Things have happened quickly for me," she noted while meeting the press in the summer of 1995. Then she added, "And they can stop as quickly as they started. But right now, I feel wonderful."

3 Taking the Next Step

On the face of it, *Party of Five* could have been an overly maudlin family drama. Created by Chris Keyser and Amy Lippman, the series presents the story of the Salingers, five siblings living in San Francisco who are trying to cope with the car-crash deaths of their parents six months earlier. The eldest, twenty-four-year-old Charlie, works as a bartender at the family restaurant, called Salingers, and now must assume the mantle of family patriarch — a role he is profoundly unprepared to fulfill. But as the only Salinger sib of legal age, it's a position he must take to keep the family together.

Bailey is the second-eldest and by far the most responsible. While Charlie may be the family leader by merit of age, Bailey is the de facto father figure by action, although that often leaves him without anyone to turn to when *he* gets frightened or needs a break. That isolation will eventually lead Bailey to seek solace in the bottle. Julia, a year younger than Bailey, is cocky and self-absorbed with an independent streak that will cause her heartache many times over. Always her parents' good girl, she reacts to becoming an orphan by adopting a "There's nobody to tell me what to do anymore, so I'm gonna walk on the wild side" persona. Eleven-year-old Claudia is the family prodigy, a gifted violinist whose emotional makeup gives her wisdom far beyond her years but who at the same time is a child missing her parents. All of the older siblings in turn are extremely protective of Owen, who hadn't yet celebrated his first birthday when the parents died.

When we first meet the Salingers, we learn that Charlie borders on being an irresponsible flake. Always a dreamer, he envisions using the insurance money from his parents' death in some questionable get-rich-quick scheme, which of course doesn't pan out, costing the family $12,000. As a result, the siblings are left without a nest egg and must struggle to make ends meet. They have only $2,500 to live on for the next four months — until the trust left behind by their parents comes through — and they must pay bills such as mortgage, groceries, plumbing, as well as a nanny for Owen. "I'm scared," Claudia says at the height of the fiscal crisis. "Why aren't they here?"

As their grief subsides and they get back to the task of living alone, the Salingers cope in their own individual ways but retain one common goal — to avoid being split up by Social Services. "The five of us have to stay together, because it matters," Bailey says. "Mom and Dad would have wanted it."

While the show was unabashedly touching, creators and writers Lippman and Keyser, who previously wrote for and executive-produced the critically lauded *Sisters*, expertly avoided turning it saccharin. Every problem rang true, as did the interaction among the siblings. And for a collaborative effort, the results are seamless. "By the time we're done, we really can't tell which one of us wrote what," says Keyser.

The two collaborators met while students at Harvard, where Lippman was in law and Keyser was already writing. Out of their friendship, which has always been platonic, grew their professional relationship. "It just worked," Keyser says of their writing. While they were still producing the series *Sisters*, Fox executives suggested a drama about orphaned kids.

Miraculously, they managed to avoid letting the show become a house party. "I think initially Fox leaned more to the fantasy element of having no parents, no limitations. I think they were expecting it to be more of a show about parties," Amy Lippman acknowledges. But what she and Keyser were interested in was "telling a story about kids who actually need to come up with rules on their own. We were thinking of all the responsibilities they would face. We thought about things like *Lord of the Flies* — kids on an island without any system of government who need to come up with something. Fox has never asked us to capitulate in any way. They've been terrific, saying, 'Do the show you want to do.'

"What makes our show different," Lippman explains, "is that there is no character who sits down with a coffee cup at the beginning of the fourth act and says, 'Honey, don't sleep with someone you don't love.' We have characters that make mistakes. I mean, really make mistakes."

While the flawless writing gives the show its depth and voice, the foundation for the appeal of *Party of Five* is the chemistry between the actors playing the Salinger siblings, a group who were, for the most part, virtual unknowns to the viewing audience. Not only do they gel into a cohesive unit, they also exude individual shine.

Not surprisingly, in the early days of the series much of the fan attention centered on the two male leads, Matthew Fox (as Charlie) and Scott Wolf (as Bailey). "We knew the guys would hit first," Lippman says. "It always works that way." From the beginning, Wolf was dubbed the "mini Tom Cruise" because of his physical similarity to the film star. "I could have done worse in this business than to be compared to Tom Cruise," Wolf would later tell Louis B. Hobson of the *Calgary Sun*. "I'm flattered beyond words. I hope someday people will go beyond my slight physical resemblance to him and talk instead about how I have the same incredible commitment to my art that he is known for in the business."

The comparison led to much teasing by his castmates. Neve affectionately called him "Mr. Personality," while Matthew Fox offered his explanation for his co-star's appeal: "It's those dimples."

Scott Wolf was born June 4, 1968, in Boston, Massachusetts, which meant that when he began in *Party of Five*, Wolf was twenty-six, ten years older than his character. "It's in the genes. If I looked my age, I'd never have had a chance to play sixteen," he says of his baby-face looks. Nicknamed Scooter as a youngster, Wolf grew up in West

Orange, New Jersey. After graduating from high school, he attended George Washington University and earned his undergraduate degree in finance, assuming his future lay in the white-collar business world — until Clint Brady, a friend of his father, suggested Wolf try his hand at acting. Obviously, Scott wasn't that gung-ho about finance, because he took up Brady's suggestion and began acting lessons at the HB Studio in New York.

When he was twenty-two, Wolf moved to Los Angeles, where he continued to study with a number of acting coaches, including Robert Carnegie and actor Jeff Goldblum at Playhouse West. Like Neve's, Scott's first television job was in a commercial — he exhorted viewers to patronize Yoshinoya Beef Bowl restaurants. He also appeared as Tony the Tiger's tennis partner in a Frosted Flakes commercial. After being turned down for a role on *Baywatch*, Wolf began picking up episodic guest spots. On *Evening Shade* he guest-starred as David Kilmer, "a quarterback with a great arm and a great smile." He also appeared twice on the teen hit *Saved by the Bell*, in two different roles.

Although he cringes good-naturedly now at these credits, Wolf also co-starred in two films prior to breaking out on *Party of Five*. The first was the dubiously named *Teenage Bonnie and Klepto Clyde*, about which he says, "You have to get started somehow." The other was *Double Dragon*, based on the arcade game of the same name, in which he played a futuristic adventurer in a post-earthquake Los Angeles. Prior to *Party of Five*, Wolf had gained a measure of notoriety by becoming seriously involved with his *Double Dragon* co-star Alyssa Milano, formerly of *Who's the Boss?*

Milano, who had shucked off her own good-girl image by playing troubled teenage seductress Amy Fisher in the CBS movie *Casualties of Love: The Long Island Lolita Story*, was effusive about her love for Wolf.

"I knew it the second I met him," Alyssa gurgled to *People* magazine. "I called my mom and told her, 'This is the man I'm gonna marry.'"

Wolf was equally smitten. "I could have asked her to marry me two weeks after we met. I'm convinced we're like two halves of the same soul."

Their romance began on-set after a game of Truth or Dare, when one matchmaking-minded crewmember dared Scott and Alyssa to kiss. Milano wrapped several days before Wolf, and when she returned to L.A. from their Cleveland location, she pined. Both admitted they worried that the magic of their location romance would fade once they resumed their daily lives. "But we looked at each other," Wolf said in *People*, "and we knew in a second that it was going to be okay."

In August 1993, Scott moved in with Milano, and that Halloween, he proposed and she accepted, with her parents' full approval. Alyssa assured everyone she knew what she was doing and made it clear theirs was more than just an extended set romance. "This is anything but that," Wolf said firmly. "You can interview us twenty-five years from now and we'll prove it."

They would call the engagement off less than a year later.

Like his character on the show, Wolf is close to his family and for several years shared a house with his brother Gary, a budding musician. Continuing the proud tradition of Hollywood nepotism, Scott helped Gary's band, Stickball, get one of their songs used on a second-season episode of *Party of Five*. As for Wolf's take on why the series has touched such a chord in so many people, he muses, "People are drawn to the show like a car accident. It's terrible to look at — horrible things are happening to other people, but you can't help but take a peek."

What he was too modest to mention was his obvious appeal to the *Tiger Beat* crowd, as evidenced by a near-riot during a personal appearance in the early days of the show. "I think the average age was sixteen. It was a mob scene which got pretty scary," he recalls. "If screaming teenagers come with success, though, then I'm more than happy to deal with that."

After his one flirtation with marriage, Wolf has remained decidedly single. His most recent involvement — with *Party of Five* co-star Paula Devicq — ended after about a year. Now past thirty,

Scott might finally be growing out of his teen-idol status and looks forward to tackling more mature roles, which he feels *Party of Five* has prepared him well for. "That was an incredible break," he says of joining the series. "It's been like getting twenty years of acting experience crammed into five years."

The other *Party of Five* heartthrob, Matthew Fox, is quite the opposite of the character he plays, who he describes this way: "Charlie has been completely overwhelmed. Between all of his responsibilities — being the oldest in the family, taking care of his four siblings, taking over the restaurant — he really has a lot on his mind. And this is a guy who began as pretty irresponsible. It's really understandable, given all he's been through. He's got a feeling of panic. It wasn't that way for me, but I'm a very different person," Fox told N.F. Mendoza of *Newsday*.

Whereas Charlie is a dreamer who finds it hard to embrace romantic commitment, Matthew has been married to Margarita Ronchi, who he met at college, for seven years and the couple have a daughter, Kyle. Fox's executive producer agrees that Matthew is not a chip off Charlie's block. "They're very different. Charlie's a free spirit, irresponsible, and can be incredibly selfish," notes Amy Lippman. "The qualities I see in Matthew from day to day are so different. He's incredibly responsible, committed to doing good work."

His work ethic is a by-product of his Wyoming upbringing. He was raised on his dad's ranch in a town he says was "a post office along a highway in between two towns that are ninety miles apart." Encouraged by his father to attend college out of state, Matthew went to Columbia University in New York on a football scholarship and majored in economics. "I was thinking I was going to work on Wall Street," he says. "I'd seen *Wall Street* and I wanted to be Charlie Sheen's character. That's the life I wanted. It seemed fascinating. But in the spring semester of my senior year, it all of a sudden hit me that was all wrong for me."

Through a friend's mother, who owned a modeling agency, Matthew began doing some commercials, which were originally "completely a side thing, just a way to make some money." After taking some acting classes, he found himself changing his life's path. "It was never like a bolt of lightning that came down and said, 'This is my dream I've always wanted to do and just never knew it.' The more I uncovered, the more passionate I got about it. Then I became really convinced it was something I wanted to do." Then, with only a few small roles to his credit, Fox was cast in *Party of Five*. But Amy Lippman points out that perhaps Fox was still hedging his bets as an actor. "On his résumé," she recalls, "he listed 'Can operate farm equipment.'" When asked about this, Fox shrugs and says, "You never know."

One of the highlights for Fox during the series' run was in 1997 when Charlie contracted Hodgkin's disease, which came on the heels of Bailey confronting his alcoholism. "Obviously, people who get emotionally involved in these characters week in and week out are just getting the stuffing knocked out of them," Fox acknowledges. "Sooner or later they're going to look at it and go, 'C'mon, give these guys a break. Let's see some happiness! Let's see some joy!'" — which Matthew does believe "our show does. We build up to happy moments. But unfortunately, those moments are sort of setups for somebody to get slammed again."

One of the least-slammed characters on *Party of Five* is Claudia, played by Lacey Chabert. Originally from Purvis, Mississippi, Lacey began performing in local theater as a child. "I always liked performing, and my sister is a singer so I liked following in her footsteps," Chabert told *Newsweek*. Then, during a family vacation to New York, nine-year-old Lacey saw that an audition was being held for *Les Miserables*. She convinced her parents to let her go and, to everyone's amazement, she got the part of young Cosette. She remained on Broadway for two years in the role. Later, she played Erica Kane's daughter Bianca in the TV soap *All My Children*.

After she was cast in *Party of Five*, the family was temporarily split, with Lacey and her mom, Julie, commuting between L.A. and Mississippi. Finally, her dad, Tony, who worked in the oil industry, was able to get a job transfer to California. Now back together,

Chabert and her family have had to cope with their own trauma when Lacey's eighteen-year-old sister, Christy, was diagnosed with a rare form of muscular dystrophy.

Like her character, Claudia, Lacey is proving to be a bit precocious. "I've asked the producers of *Party of Five* several times to let me direct an episode," she told Jefferson Graham of USA *Today*. "They just laughed. They said to come back after I turn eighteen. But I'm really serious about this."

Growing up on a television show in front of millions of people year after year can be a strange experience. When one particular episode called for Claudia to kiss a boy, Lacey's mom felt usurped as a parent. "I was really unhappy with the script," Julie Chabert admitted to *TV Guide*'s Mary Murphy. "I mean, she's never done that in real life. I was going, 'Oh, my gosh! An older boy kissing my daughter!' I couldn't watch because it was my thirteen-year-old."

Like a lot of other teens her age, Lacey admits to having had a mad crush on co-star Scott Wolf when the series began. "I was in love with him at first," she told Murphy. "I used to think, maybe one day he will wait for me. But as we got to know each other, suddenly we became best buddies. You can't really marry your best friend. So I gave up on that. Not to mention that he did meet someone else."

While she may have lost her puppy love for Wolf, Lacey doesn't lack passion in her life. "I love what I do. I want to do features. I want to go to college when I am older. I want to go to Paris to film school. That would be awesome."

Such vision has prompted producer Lippman to wryly note, "Sometimes, I think Lacey is older than I am."

During *Party of Five*'s hiatus in spring 1995, Neve was in England working opposite Patrick Stewart on an ABC television movie, *The Canterville Ghost*. Based on the story by Oscar Wilde, *The Canterville Ghost* tells the tale of a sixteenth-century spirit who does his best to scare away an American family that has moved into his castle.

Stewart played the ghostly Sir Simon Canterville while Neve was cast as Virginia Otis, the teenager who befriends him.

Wilde's story had been adapted twice before to feature films, including one starring 1940s top moppet Margaret O'Brien. Most critics were kind to ABC's small-screen effort and Campbell's performance in it. Critic Terry Kelleher noted, "Campbell is appealing in her own right, and (director Sydney) MacCartney further advances her cause by allotting the young actress even more moist-eyed closeups than the little O'Brien lass got back in '44. The supernatural effects are a bit much when Virginia enters the 'realm of darkness' to plead for Sir Simon before the angel of death, but we tend to buy her growing devotion to the perturbed old spirit. In fact, we'd sooner she ran off to the next world with him than remained in this one to share romance with a boring duke her own age."

Neve had similar feelings of affection for Stewart, although of a more professional nature. "I love Patrick Stewart. He's an incredibly inspiring actor. And if at his age, I have the body of work that he's accomplished I will be very happy with my career."

While on location for the telefilm, Neve was joined by boyfriend Jeff Colt, and in an impulsive moment, the couple married. When Colt had first proposed to Neve, she admitted it was quite a shock. "I was twenty-one and had sworn I would never get married young because my parents did and it didn't work out," she commented. "But then I realized that I had to look at my situation separately. Jeff and I had been together five years and you can only be so sure. You either do it or you don't. I felt that if I wasn't willing to take the next step, why be in the relationship at all?"

There was also the matter of Colt's immigration status. Jeff wanted to join Campbell in Los Angeles, where *Party of Five* was taped, but he couldn't stay there without a green card. As Neve's co-star Michael Goorjian, who played Campbell's boyfriend Justin on the show, explains, "If they didn't marry, they couldn't be together."

So on April 4, 1995, Neve and Jeff were married in a ceremony at the Registry Office of Westminster, near Wimbledon, England. They invited only thirteen guests, all of whom were working on the film. "No, no family," she tells *TV Guide*. "I love my family very much, and that was obviously a difficult decision. My immediate family are incredible . . . but not in the same room, you know?"

After the telefilm wrapped, Neve and Jeff went on a honeymoon to Paris, Venice, and Zurich. But even in the earliest days of her marriage, when most newlyweds are blinded by bliss, Campbell's head steered clear of any clouds. "Jeff and I both have a very realistic view of marriage," she says, speaking carefully. "You try as hard as you can, and you love each other as much as you can, and you hope to grow together. You hope that divorce is not an option. But if you're miserable, you know, together, then why continue?"

As she told *People* magazine, "If we grow apart, that's a circumstance we'll deal with."

4 Some Noise of Her Own

Despite the critical praise being heaped on *Party of Five*, the sad fact was, nobody was watching. Or, more accurately, not enough people were watching to generate the kind of ratings that keep a show on the air. So as the first season neared its end, few of the show's most ardent supporters really believed *Party of Five* would be renewed — except producers Keyser and Lippman. "I think Fox is really invested in this show," Chris Keyser asserted. "They want it back." Even though John Matoian, then president of programming, pledged his support — "Chris and Amy have done a great job at taking what could have been a really depressing show and making it something far greater than that. It's a show I believe in." — all signs still pointed to the early demise of another quality show.

In an effort to help build ratings, Fox had moved the show in January from its original time on Monday to a post-*Beverly Hills 90210* slot. But during the February sweeps, the series was massacred competing against the specials offered up by the other networks. "We were up against the Grammys and a *Roseanne* special," Keyser lamented at the time. "I hope that's the last of it."

If the show's time was up, the producers made sure it would go out with a bang. In the last episode of the season, aired in March 1995, one of the recurring characters, Bailey's girlfriend Jill, dies from a cocaine overdose while a gay character confronts barriers in trying to adopt a child. Also, Charlie gets engaged. Keyser and Lippman had set themselves up perfectly for another season from a dramatic point of view. But now all they could do was sit back and wait to find out whether or not they would be picked up.

A typically negative bunch, critics began writing the show's obituaries as soon as the final episode aired. Then *USA Today* television writer Matt Roush announced there was "little cause to celebrate at tonight's going-away for *Party of Five*. The season-ender has it all: tragedy, romance, joy, moments of tenderness and power and humor. Or maybe it doesn't have enough — of what it takes to succeed in a meaner, cruder time. The ratings: so very poor for something so very rich. Maybe Fox will startle us all and give the show yet another chance. Only then would I break out the party favors."

For their part, the actors refused to believe the worst. "Everyone feels pretty good about our chances," Scott Wolf asserted. However, Matthew Fox admitted to not understanding how the show could be ranked 87th in the ratings. "I can't figure out why the numbers aren't very good," he said, "because everyone I know watches the show."

Repeating the mantra of most dramas, Amy Lippman pointed out that "shows like this need time to find an audience." And looking for any positive sign, Keyser added, "We're not in a significantly different place than *90210*, *Melrose Place*, and *The X-Files* were in their first years."

While the Fox network may have not interfered with Keyser and Lippman's vision of the show, some of the promos for *Party of Five* in the spring of 1995 showed that unmistakable Fox attitude. One ad flashed a shot of a shirtless Matthew Fox, while a voice intoned, "*Melrose* doesn't have the only bad boy on Monday night." When asked her opinion about the spots, Campbell was pragmatic. "The way the show's being advertised really has nothing to do with what it's about. But if it's going to draw in people who watch *90210* and *Melrose*, then that's a good thing."

The cast had also done their part over the course of the year, with Fox, Wolf, and Campbell going wherever they were pointed to promote the series — talk shows, personal appearances, celebrity events. And it was when meeting the public that they became aware of the loyalty of the viewers they did have. "At this mall appearance in New York, we were expecting a smattering of applause, and for people not to know who we were," Wolf remembers. "But it was out of control." Being the object of teenage desire was "really, really strange," admitted Fox. "Sometimes I feel as if I'm on the outside, watching, and I can't believe it's me signing autographs."

Neve also got a taste of teen mania for the show. "It was trippy. It was trippy having thousands of teenage girls screaming and crying and grabbing. I mean, all of a sudden you feel like a rock star and then you realize that you're not, that you're in people's living rooms once a week, and they sit on their couches and they watch you so they feel that they know you. It's understandable that they get excited, but it's overwhelming. It's an odd experience, because I think all of us, as actors, think about what it is to be famous and what it is to be a celebrity and what will that experience be, and there's really no describing it when it happens. Because the truth is, when I'm in those situations, it just seems absurd to me. Not that they're being ridiculous, but that I am simply *me*. I'm still this little girl who was, you know, really insecure and didn't fit in at school and who was really unpopular and considered the ugliest in the class. And then I'll stand in a room with thousands of people screaming and whatever — it's overwhelming. It's definitely an overwhelming experience because I don't see myself as that."

Promoting a show to the masses can be an exhausting, disorienting experience, as Neve related to David Kronke of the *L.A. Times*. "I've been to many states in this country, and I can't even tell you which ones they are. When I travel, people ask, 'Have you been here before?' and I say, 'I think I may have. I recognize the airport, I've seen that mall before.' But you don't see anything else! You fly out that day and fly back that night, and all you see are thousands of people who want your autograph."

Keyser and Lippman made calls to critics part of their daily routine, it seemed, having no qualms about asking for just one more story about the series. "The press that we got helped us a lot in the first season," acknowledges Lippman. "I think Fox needed to feel that if they weren't getting the immediate reward of fantastic ratings that there was another reason to keep the show on the air." For as nerve-wracking a time as it was, the live-or-die experience helped season the young producers. "The learning curve was very steep. The stakes felt really high. It was a really exciting time. The actors felt it as well," recalls Lippman.

In May 1995, to the surprise of many, Fox renewed *Party of Five* for a second season. But even that didn't stop the speculation that the series' days were numbered, in part because the network had only ordered half a season's worth of episodes. Many theorized that Fox was simply using *Party of Five* to fill the time slot that would eventually go to the planned new David E. Kelly show, *The Pastor's Wife*, expected to air in January. But neither the creators nor the actors could worry about what might happen in the future. They knew only that they were living to see another prime-time day. And, seemingly all of a sudden, the cast members' stars shone a little brighter. Neve, who had splurged and bought herself a Volkswagen Cabriolet — "I went all out" — was being touted as one of the bright new faces of television. *Time* magazine called her "tv's most believable teenager," listing her side by side with Bart Simpson's feisty, forgetful granddad, Abraham J. Simpson, as one of six bright lights in the vast wasteland of network television. While honored by the accolade, Neve put the praise in typical Campbell perspective. "People started calling up and congratulating me," she told one interviewer, "and all I could think of was, 'My picture's next to Grandpa Simpson.' I mean, Grandpa Simpson's awesome, but you can't take it too seriously."

On the set, the cast members had grown into a family of their own, with good-natured teasing and affectionate ribbing signaling their increasing closeness. Neve was given the nickname Foghorn. "It's true," Campbell smiles. "There was a scene in the first season where I went" — she gives a laugh that sounds like a goose honking — "out of nowhere for no reason whatsoever. They said, 'Cut!' and everybody just looked at me and said, 'What was that?' So now I'm Foghorn. I laugh like that every once in a while when I'm uncomfortable."

And, Neve points out, others have their own eccentricities. "Scott

Wolf snorts," she laughingly reveals. "He does this, like, swallowing thing, this really awful snort, like he's bringing up phlegm. It drives me nuts. It's absolutely disgusting. I always razz him about that one."

In fact, Campbell spent a lot of time teasing her teen idol co-star. "It's so funny when I get letters from little girls saying, 'Oh, you should date Scott Wolf!' Little do they know I'm married. But on the other hand, to me, you know, he's my brother. I think of him as my brother. So to me, it's just gross even thinking of him in that sense. I don't know, because I don't try to get to Scott. I usually insult Scott a lot. My cynical or sarcastic sense of humor comes out."

In the early days of the series, Campbell and her castmates often went out socially, to each other's homes for dinner and company. "When I came out from Canada everyone was really wonderful because I was alone and didn't have friends out here." But as the series became more known, the actors found it more difficult to wander about unnoticed. "It's a bummer to get interrupted in the middle of a nice meal, you know?" Campbell noted.

When the series' second-season opener aired in September 1995, fans were pleased to see that *Party of Five* hadn't undergone a major overhaul. Neve's character was now a high school junior torn between her boyfriend Justin and the troubled Griffin. In retrospect, it seems obvious that eventually bad boy Griffin would win out — after all, *Party of Five* thrived on pain and suffering. But at the time, most viewers probably thought Julia would come to her senses and stay with Justin, played by Michael Goorjian, who might not have traditional leading-man looks, but makes up for it with a highly developed passion for his work.

A multifaceted performer, Michael Goorjian decided early the key to longevity in Hollywood was diversity, so he pursues acting, writing, directing, producing, and even choreography with equal determination. "It's become fashionable to do it all," says Goorjian, "but I certainly don't do it for the sake of being popular. I do it because it makes sense to work on things you enjoy."

Those who knew him growing up might have expected Goorjian to end up a scientist or a doctor. The son of a mathematician father who works for NASA and a nurse mother, Michael is the only one in his family to even consider a profession in entertainment. But Goorjian has always followed his own unique view of the world. His first dabble in the arts was with a San Francisco performance group called Maldoror Productions. The group's name came from a French surrealist novel Michael credits with impacting on his creativity.

Although not exactly a household name, when Goorjian joined *Party of Five* as "the best friend and romantic interest to actress Neve Campbell's Julia," as he describes Justin, he was well-known within the industry and had just won an Emmy for Outstanding Supporting Actor in a Miniseries or Special for his performance in the CBS telefilm *David's Mother*. He has also appeared in several feature films, including *Hard Rain*, *Leaving Las Vegas*, *Forever Young*, and *Chaplin*, as well as receiving critical notice for *SLC Punks*, which co-starred Matthew Lillard, who would later co-star with Neve in *Scream*.

Despite his success in mainstream projects, anything alternative seems to appeal to Goorjian most. "I could easily buy a big house and a nice car, but I choose to reinvest the money I make on not-so-desirable projects," he says, calling such projects "the work I really enjoy doing." His family has been completely supportive of Michael's path. "My parents like to joke that they know I'm still alive because they can turn on *Party of Five* from time to time and see me on TV," the young actor says. "We all sort of learned about the ups and downs of this business together," including the realization that "If you want to do something, don't just talk about it. Do it."

That was advice Matthew Fox's character seemed to be taking, with Charlie busy planning his wedding — which, of course, wouldn't go smoothly. Bailey, for his part, was about to get a new love interest of his own, Julia's friend Sarah, played by Jennifer

Neve and Michael Goorjian

LISA ROSE / GLOBE PHOTOS

Love Hewitt, who at one point began to overshadow Campbell as the *Party of Five* pin-up girl. Before the television year was out, Hewitt would seemingly be everywhere. She had been performing for nearly her entire life, starting when she was a toddler. According to Hewitt family lore, when Jennifer was only four years old, she wandered away from her mom and older brother at a restaurant/club and ended up onstage singing an impromptu rendition of "Help Me Make It Through the Night."

That song selection might not have been as unusual as it seems at first glance. Hewitt's parents, Tom and Pat, divorced in 1979, when Love was a six-month-old infant, and she and her older brother Todd were raised by Pat. Although born in Waco, Texas, Love was raised in Killeen, a small town north of Austin, Texas, where her mom worked as a speech pathologist. But it was apparent to Pat early on that her daughter was destined to be elsewhere. Maybe it was her name — anyone christened "Love" had better be something special.

"I was named after my mom's best friend in college," Hewitt explains. "She was like five-eleven, long blond hair past her butt, big blue eyes, freckles, and an hourglass figure. She was the most beautiful woman my mom had ever seen, and they were so close that my mom said if she ever had a little girl, she would name her Love. So when I was born she of course named me Love — even though I came out, like, five-three, brown hair, half an hourglass figure, and completely different looking."

She was renamed Jennifer Love when her brother, then nine, felt his little sister might prefer a "normal" name when she grew up and suggested Jennifer, the name of a neighborhood girl on whom he had a crush. His concern was unfounded — to this day she prefers to be called Love.

After her daughter's nightclub "debut," Pat enrolled Love in dance classes, where she studied tap, jazz, and ballet. Seemingly driven to perform, the youngster also sang at local livestock shows. "I never really fit in where I lived in Texas," observes Hewitt. "I would host and direct and star in these little plays, even though my friends never really wanted to do it. I just always thought there was something wrong with *them*." While still in Texas, Love was voted a "Living Doll" in a state beauty pageant, and a short time later she became a member of the Texas Show Team, the highlight coming when she accompanied the troupe on a performance tour of Russia and Denmark.

"I thought everybody's little girl could do what she did," admits Pat. But others made it clear her daughter was definitely out of the ordinary. Finally, a combination of Love's pleas and a local talent scout's referral to a manager friend in Los Angeles convinced Pat to give her daughter a chance to pursue her career. In 1989, on Love's tenth birthday, Pat packed up her family and moved to Los Angeles. Within weeks, Love had been hired to appear on the Disney Channel variety show *Kids Incorporated*, playing Robin. "When I first heard Love sing, I was blown away," said Reg Powell, the show's musical director. One of the other young performers was an already handsome boy named Scott Wolf, who played twins.

Love left the show after two years to work on a short-lived Fox sitcom, *Shaky Ground*. During this time, she had also become a commercial mainstay, appearing in over twenty television spots, including ads for Mattel, Barbie, Mrs. Smith's Pies, Circuit City, and Chex cereal. She also participated in the infamous L.A. Gear print and television campaign featuring Michael Jackson.

Love's career took off so unexpectedly fast that Pat felt compelled to put her own career on hold in order to maintain some sanity in her daughter's life. Until Love was eighteen, she had a 10 PM curfew during the week and maintained an A average in school. "Mom is a big reason why Love is who she is," says brother Todd, now a Dallas chiropractor. Love is equally devoted to Pat: "My mom is very strong, very funny, and sees the good side of everything. She's positive even when life is bad."

After appearing in the 1992 film *Munchie*, Hewitt showed off her vocal skills in the *Dance! Work Out With Barbie* exercise video, in which she sang all of the songs heard in the background. That led to an unusual debut album. Recorded on Medlac Records, *Love Songs* was released only in Japan.

Love's next breakthrough came when she was cast opposite

Whoopie Goldberg in *Sister Act 2* in 1993. "I played Margaret," Love says, "who was the kind of girl who is afraid people won't like her if she's not pretty. She cops a very bad attitude and is never seen without her compact of makeup — that is, until Sister Mary Clarence wakes her up and shows her what love is all about."

Although she was still virtually unknown to the general public, Love was earning notice among the Hollywood powers that be, particularly television executives. In 1994, she landed what was considered a plum role in ABC's drama *Byrds of Paradise*, playing former *thirtysomething* star Timothy Busfield's rebellious fifteen-year-old daughter. Despite the network's high hopes for the series, *Byrds* fell flat, running only half a season before low ratings and on-set controversy (Busfield was accused of inappropriate behavior toward a female crew member) caused the network to pull the plug.

Typically, Love avoided any negative residue from the experience and immediately afterward signed a contract to record her American debut album on Atlantic Records. *Let's Go Bang*, a mix of dance songs and ballads, was released in 1995 and featured a song co-written by Hewitt.

After another short-lived series, ABC's *McKenna*, Love was hired for *Party of Five*. "When I auditioned for the part, I knew I could play her," Hewitt says. "I had no questions about Sarah. I knew how to play her instantly because we're exactly alike in so many ways." Love's character was introduced in the second-season premiere as a potential love interest for Bailey. "Being the new cast member was a bit weird at first," Hewitt admits. "I've known Scott Wolf for a really long time so I wasn't really nervous about seeing him again, but I was worried about the rest of the cast. You can't help but worry about being accepted and being kind of like the third wheel, on the outside of all the personal jokes and stuff like that.

"But from the first day, they included me in their jokes and took the time to explain what they meant. They really made me feel welcome. Not only did they give each other hugs in the morning, but they included me in those also. They've made me feel so comfortable, I feel like I had been on the show since the beginning."

Many, in fact, credit Love for helping get *Party of Five* over the ratings hump by adding an element previously missing from the show's emotional mix. And Sarah and Bailey's tortured relationship — they eventually get together, but he screws things up by being unfaithful, then realizes what an idiot he's been and tries to get Sarah back, yadda, yadda, yadda — was addictive among the show's young viewers.

Despite being the poster girl for teenage heartbreak, Love says this role is her favorite. "First of all, sometimes I say, 'Wow, I'm the luckiest teenager alive — kissing an older man every day and getting paid for it!'" she jokes. "And Sarah's the coolest person you'd ever want to meet — very smart, quick, and witty. On *Byrds of Paradise* and *McKenna*, I played the teen angst characters. You know, the kid going through rough times, yelling at the parents and getting really frustrated. Sarah seems to have it all together, though. She has it all in perspective and she's really down to earth, really sweet. She has an incredible head on her shoulders."

Many have said the same about Love. "Love has a teenager's personality and a grownup's professional perspective," says Keyser, who was in on the decision to cast Hewitt for what was originally envisioned as only a handful of episodes. "You can't imagine that someone who's that young can be so professional."

That dedication to her profession didn't come without sacrifices in her personal life. The girl who is so beloved by *Party of Five* fans was often an outcast in school while growing up. "In junior high school, the kids thought I was a nerd," Love says. "In their eyes, I was weird because I did things differently and I didn't go to parties. I've never been to a high-school or a junior high-school party with people my age."

For all of the notoriety she's achieved, Hewitt remains surprisingly unaffected by it all. "It's so shocking and still so overwhelming when people recognize me. It's crazy, because I look up to people like that. I mean, if I were to meet Winona Ryder, I would probably pee in my pants!" She laughs. "I would literally be speechless. So when people look at me that way, it's so weird!"

As for her own rising star, Hewitt takes a wait-and-see approach, choosing not to look so far ahead that she misses out on her current good fortune. "I don't know what the future will hold," she says. "I kind of like not knowing what's going to happen next. It makes it exciting."

While it seemed as if Love were going to be the big breakout star from the cast, Neve Campbell was about to make some noise of her own.

5 Witching Hour

Whatever else one may say about Neve Campbell, there can be no disputing her work ethic. While some actors may have been content to take it easy before starting the grueling schedule an hour-long television drama demands, Campbell filled her remaining hiatus time by working on a low-budget 1996 thriller called *The Craft*, directed by Andrew Fleming. Filmed on location in the Los Angeles area, the movie starred Neve, Robin Tunney, Fairuza Balk, and Rachel True as Bonnie, Sarah, Rochelle, and Nancy, respectively — four alienated high school girls who conjure the powers of witchcraft to settle scores with their peers.

Initially, when Bonnie, Rochelle, and Nancy try their hands at the black arts, nothing much happens because they need a fourth to complete their circle of power — one witch is needed for each of the four points of the compass. "We are misfits and don't fit in with everyone else, so together we form our own clique," says Neve. Conveniently, their missing link appears in the guise of Sarah, who has been suicidal in the past. That there's something out of the ordinary about Sarah is made clear in the opening sequence of the film, which shows Sarah and her family moving into a dilapidated mansion that looks like a New Orleans transplant. Just before Sarah leaves to attend her first day at St. Benedict's Academy, a Catholic high school ensconced in a tony section of L.A., a stranger comes to the door, holding a snake.

As the new kid on the block, Sarah is looked upon as an outsider, although she feels a tingling of hope when one of the school's football heroes asks her out. But when she refuses his sexual advances and he begins to spread nasty tales about her, Sarah joins the would-be coven and shows that she actually has some abilities of her own. With her telekinetic powers up and running, Sarah brings the cliquey coven to life. Fortified by some wine, and toting various magic ingredients picked up at the local witch boutique, the foursome go into the woods, form a circle, and get down to the business of casting spells.

Campbell's character, Bonnie, has terrible facial scars from being burned as a child. "She was in a fiery car accident and burned very badly, and she was left with horrible scars all over her body," Neve explains. "So she feels very insecure about herself and her body because of this trauma. She's very interested in people, but never quite fits in. The rest of the girls also have dark secrets which set them apart from the other kids at school. But with her newly found powers, Bonnie is able to heal the scars that have caused her to be the butt of agonizing taunting in school, while Rochelle, a young black woman, wreaks revenge on an *uber*-blonde peer who slings racial slurs at her. And the ringleader of the witchy quartet — known at their school as the Bitches of Eastwick — is Nancy, a specter of punk alienation. With her magic, she sees to it that her mother's abusive boyfriend dies, leaving behind an insurance windfall.

Initially, once they see their magic actually works, the girls are taken aback and unsure of what to do with it. But the sensation of power is too seductive to ignore and soon they are flaunting their prowess, striding through the corridors of St. Benedict's Academy shattering light bulbs and mirrors with psychic missiles. Of course, the power they possess inevitably turns corruptive, with Nancy becoming the bad seed, leaving it up to Sarah to stop her from inflicting any more havoc upon those around her.

Although *The Craft* opened at number one and scored a modest success at the box office, critics were split in their assessment of the film, with most feeling that the promising beginning degenerated to schlock horror-film antics at the end, when Sarah and Nancy face off in their good vs. evil showdown. But the performers mostly received praise.

Roger Ebert said, "If it's hard to imagine anyone much over high school age getting a kick out of all of this numbing violence and terror, it must be said that *The Craft* is well-made with a hard-driving pace. It places heavy demands on its four lead actresses, who come through in impressive fashion. Director and co-writer Andrew Fleming makes sure he and his stars deliver the goods."

Campbell thought it "was very interesting working in a film that was about witchcraft. Something that I found intriguing is that we had an actual witch on the set with us, talking with us and coaching us through the scenes." She later told *Australian TV Hits* that while filming the movie, the actresses "were all sent books on witchcraft. There's nothing to be afraid of," Neve explained. "What I learned about witchcraft is that it's about strength within your own soul and it's the powers of nature — earth, air, water, and fire. It's not really about evil. Black witchcraft can be about evil. But there *are* other witchcrafts."

And as it turned out, not all witches were equally thrilled about *The Craft*. Pat Devon, the on-set witch, "told us that there was an entire coven of witches who had put a curse on the movie because they were upset we might commercialize witchcraft or put it in a wrong light," Neve revealed to Jenny Cooney of *Australian TV Week*. Whether you believe in that or not, it's a scary thing in itself to be told."

With that thought planted in the actresses' minds, it's not surprising that they began to see strange occurrences around them, such as when a butterfly fluttered among them for an entire scene. Okay, not the stuff of *The Exorcist*, but weird if you're already a bit jumpy. Then there was the time the bats came a-calling during a scene being shot on the beach, where the four girls were gathered around a fire intoning an incantation.

"It was the middle of the night and it had taken hours to set up this scene and get the fire going," recalls Neve. "When the director called 'Action,' the tide came up and put the fire out and swept all our candles down the beach. Then suddenly these bats came out of nowhere and flew overhead, which was frightening. The whole thing was really creepy."

For the scenes in which Bonnie's scars were visible, Campbell had to spend long hours in the makeup chair. "Man, the days that I had to wear those scars were such a nightmare because we were already shooting," she says. "My days would be about eighteen hours long because I'd go in five hours before the rest of the crew to have my makeup put on. It isn't very good for the skin. It takes about an hour and a half to take off because they have to slowly peel it away without ripping your skin."

But besides the trying hours spent on the set, shooting was tough for Neve because it meant being away from her new husband. "I had just had my honeymoon and then flew back here and did *The Craft*," she says. Then she adds, "It was a good experience, though, because it really is about four girls becoming empowered, although they abuse it and take it to another level."

After *The Craft* wrapped, and as she prepared to return to the second season of *Party of Five*, Neve seemed almost optimistic about how her life and career were going. "The work seems to be coming fairly consistently, which I'm ecstatic about," she said. "I'm tired because it's been long hours and non-stop, but I'm very happy to be working so much. So I really can't complain."

At the time, about her only gripe was that she was discovering that convincingly playing a teenager on television and in the movies could give rise to some curious real-life situations. "I was in a bar and had shown my ID, but the people in the bar kept saying to the waitress, 'She's not old enough, you have to kick her out,'" Neve recalls. "The waitress came up to me and said, 'I've seen your ID, but I've been told you're sixteen, so you're going to have to leave.' I had to convince her it was ridiculous that people thought I was the character! I said, 'Look, I'm wearing a wedding ring!' So she finally gave in and let me stay."

Although at times it seemed a painfully slow process, *Party of Five* began to show signs of increasing ratings strength, relatively speaking. It was still ranked in the lower third of all shows and continued to struggle to build its audience, but the fans it did have were positively rabid about the series. In January 1996, *Party of Five* received a much-needed and greatly appreciated boost from the Hollywood Foreign Press, a group of about eighty foreign journalists who dole out the popular but occasionally suspect Golden Globe Awards — suspect because there are many within Hollywood who believe the Golden Globes are often little more than a popularity contest, with the winners being those actors who most successfully wine and dine the Foreign Press members.

But for a struggling television show like *Party of Five*, winning the Golden Globe for Best Drama Series was a major injection of Neilsen blood. At the time, the awards ceremony was the most exciting, glamorous event Campbell had ever attended. "That night was extremely surreal. I met so many people. It was a trip, because as I was walking up to the stage, someone tapped me on the shoulder and said, 'Congratulations.' I was like, 'Thanks.' And when I turned around, it was Tom Hanks! Later on, Brad Pitt told Lacey that he loves our show and was so happy we won. I was talking to John Travolta and I introduced my husband and I was like, 'John, this is my husband, Jeff,' and then I thought, 'Omigod! I just called him John!' It was amazing to realize that these people watch the show and know who we are! It was obviously a very thrilling experience."

Thanks to the Golden Globe, the continued positive critical reception to the show, and improved ratings, *Party of Five* was picked up for a third season. In keeping with the show's themes, life for the Salingers continued to be a series of crises to overcome, with the problems changing as the siblings matured. "The characters are definitely growing up," agreed Christopher Keyser. Campbell added, "People really relate to us. The writers have always been less interested in the glamour and look of the show than in the emotions and growth of the characters."

Scott Wolf believed the series just kept getting dramatically better: "As the show has moved off into relationships and into the lives of each individual, it has gotten a lot more accessible and a lot more watchable." And, occasionally, controversial. One of the more publicized storylines had Neve's character, Julia, find out she is pregnant. Realistically, Julia considers an abortion. "Her pregnancy was a risk for the producers but necessary, considering how irresponsible she was," Campbell tells Bernard Weintraub in *Cosmopolitan*. But instead of an abortion, Julia winds up having a very convenient miscarriage. "In the original script, she was going to have an abortion, but then the producers felt her decision was too controversial. Miscarriage was an easy way out. I thought it was just silly."

Silly but network-safe. Interestingly, because *Party of Five* had already earned its credentials as a solid drama, instead of being blasted because its lead teenage character got pregnant, the show was hailed as a vanguard of social responsibility. And in response to the one or two critics who complained the series was beginning to show splotches of *90210*-ism, Keyser insisted, "It's not a sexy show from a point of view of showing bodies. We're careful to make sure that we are relatively conservative. Giving speeches about why sex is wrong or abstinence is right won't affect anyone. Watching a sixteen-year-old going through something like that is more likely to have a positive effect. I hope it's O.K. to say that our characters make the mistake so you don't have to."

And, of course, Julia wasn't the only Salinger destined to sing "Nobody knows the trouble I've seen." "Every relationship on the show will be called into question," promised Keyser. "When you're sixteen or seventeen, you don't stay with the same people forever, so our cast won't stay with the same people. All of the relationships will be up in the air."

That very reality sometimes had Lacey Chabert worried. "I think it's a good family show, but what happens when everyone goes off to college? When everyone gets on with their lives?" she asked. "Sometimes that's a little scary."

When the cast and crew filmed the final episode of the first season, nobody had known whether that would be the series' swan song. That was not the case for the final episode of the second season, which gave the writers additional leeway in how to end the show — when a show is definitely coming back, more unanswered questions can be left for resolution the following season. Keeping the viewers dangling brings them back.

The episode that concluded the second season in some ways brought the family full circle. In the beginning, Charlie had been a reluctant father figure who over the next year got his act together enough to propose marriage to girlfriend Kirsten. But after getting cold feet and calling the wedding off, he had reverted to his less responsible ways and was now on the brink of losing the lease to the family restaurant to the building's new owner, a vengeful spurned lover of Charlie's. Then, if he doesn't already feel badly enough, he learns Kirsten is marrying someone else.

On the other end, Bailey, who is about to graduate from high school, is weary of being the family rock and plans to go away to college, leaving behind both family and girlfriend Sarah. But, of course, in the end, his inherent selflessness will win out. Julia, still adjusting to the trauma of her unwanted pregnancy, is ready to break up with longtime boyfriend Justin and be on her own awhile.

As USA *Today* critic Matt Roush noted, "The family that cries together thrives together. With love in ruins and the family business on the ropes, the Salingers have a bawl in tonight's emotionally overwrought two-hour finale. A good time is had by no one but the hanky-holding fan."

Even if *Party of Five* still lacked enviable ratings, it had something that in many ways was more important. It had respectability, a quality always yearned for by networks and producers, who spend much of their time excusing or defending their programming. So when the Academy of Television Arts and Sciences proposed a new Emmy category, the President's Award, the networks entered into a veritable chess game, vying to get questionable programs nominated. The award was created as a way for the frequently criticized TV industry to show off its most responsible programming and honor the special, movie, or series that "best explores social or educational issues."

Obviously, that little description meant different things to different producers. Eighty-seven programs were submitted for nomination.

By comparison, categories such as best comedy get about fifty nominees. The submissions for the award ranged from ABC's *Beatles Anthology* to a Nickelodeon antismoking special to "The One With the Lesbian Wedding" *Friends* episode.

Coincidentally, *Party of Five* also aired an episode that touched upon the theme of lesbianism, but in a much more low-key fashion. In the episode, a woman makes a pass at Julia, who at first is shaken up, but then comes to her senses. Campbell says she liked being able to show viewers that who you love isn't a big deal. "Like race, black or white — I see absolutely no difference," she tells *Genre* magazine. "Because for me it's just such a reality: You are human, I am human, let's try to accept one another for whatever we are. It was actually kind of weird for me to flip out about it. I felt like slapping Julia and saying, 'Relax!'

"Actually, one of my girlfriends came out after she and I had been friends for a couple of years. And it was really funny because she was so nervous about telling me. And when she told me I was like, 'OK, you got a beer?' It doesn't change who you are and what you mean to me."

With no specific guideline to follow, it was inevitable that submissions for the President's Award would be all over the map. "The President's Award is one of those things that is in the eye of the beholder," understated awards director John Leverence. "There's an extremely broad range of submissions, and it's really going to be interesting who gets nominated."

Party of Five, which surely seemed like a no-brainer to submit, found itself in the center of a disagreement between its studio, Columbia Tri-Star TV, and NBC. The peacock network pressured Columbia to nominate *Mad About You*, but the studio execs refused, saying the show wasn't appropriate. Instead, Columbia submitted only one episode from one series — the *Party of Five* in which Neve's Julia considers an abortion.

In May 1996, *The Craft* opened, and for the first time people were forced to consider the possibility that Neve might have genuine big-screen presence. While many television stars get an opportunity to appear in films, most of those efforts do little to enhance their big-screen futures or burn up the box office. Campbell seemed sharply aware of the low percentage of young actors who successfully make the transition. "Well, I really hope I'm not the face of the minute," she admitted. "I want to last at least for a few months, so I am trying to expand myself to different kinds of roles."

What seemed to amuse Campbell, though, was having to constantly relive a high-school experience on camera. "It's kind of wonderful," she noted in *Genre*. "For me, being able to play out Julia and have these love triangles — these are things I never had. So it's a way for me to live that out without having to go back."

The next project Neve would work on during her hiatus would also take her back to high school — and into the annals of horror-film legend.

6 Neve: A Reluctant Horror Princess

There's a long and fine tradition in America horror cinema of putting oversexed teens in jeopardy at the hands of psychotic killers. Perhaps the granddaddy of this sub-genre was *The Texas Chainsaw Massacre*, in which a leather-masked, chainsaw-toting madman hacked a score of teens to death. Almost inevitably, the first casualties are that hormone-driven couple who sneak away from the group to indulge in carnal desires, the de facto lesson being that teenage sex kills. Over the years, in countless drive-in-quality horror flicks, the stereotypes were finely honed. Anyone who went to a slasher film pretty much knew what to expect; the fun was watching it played out in all its fake gory glory.

The formula began to change with John Carpenter's seminal *Halloween*. While it had the vulnerable heroine and enough blood to supply a Red Cross station, its phantom-like killer gave even jaded horror-movie aficionados a new chill. But in Hollywood, once someone comes up with something unique, copycat producers and creators take the idea and run it to death. After *Halloween* came the endless franchises of *Nightmare on Elm Street*, in which the dream-dwelling Freddy Krueger knocked off his victims faster than a skeet shooter downing clay pigeons, and *Friday the 13th*, with its goalie-masked Jason. With each sequel, the movies' impact lessened until they became unwitting caricatures of themselves — just like their villains. And then along came Kevin Williamson, the right man at the right time to reconstruct the horror genre.

Like that of many other would-be screenwriters, Williamson's early career consisted of a few heady highs tempered by many more depressing lows. The son of a fisherman raised in rural North Carolina, Williamson knew as a teenager he wanted to write and resolutely refused to accept the opinion of a high-school English teacher who told him he'd never make it. "She said my grammar was terrible and I was just a kid from the sticks who'd never be a writer," he recalls vividly. "She paralyzed me for a while."

He later came to L.A. and was succeeding at being a failed actor when he used that humiliating experience as the basis for his first screenplay, a black comedy called *Killing Mrs. Tingle*. "The best moment of my career was printing out *Mrs. Tingle* for the first time, binding it with three brads. I jumped up and down on my bed for an hour because I'd done something I'd been told I couldn't do." To his supreme satisfaction, the script was optioned and Williamson used his first real money to pay off some college loans and get himself a nice car.

But a script being optioned and being filmed are two very separate issues. As *Mrs. Tingle* collected dust on an office shelf somewhere, Williamson fretted that his screenwriting career might wind up very brief indeed. To pay his bills he worked as an office temp, house-sat, and looked after pets. Then, spurred on by desperation, Williamson took a trip to Palm Springs, rented a motel room, and wrote the first draft for what he then called, simply, *Scary Movie*.

"I got the idea two and a half years ago from watching a Barbara Walters special on the Gainesville murders," he says. "I was broke, house-sitting for a friend to pay him back for money he'd lent me for groceries, and I was scaring the hell out of myself. I thought I heard a noise. I walked the house with a butcher knife and a phone, and called a friend while I searched the place. We got into this huge discussion, testing each other on horror movies. And that's how *Scream* was born." Ironically, though, Kevin isn't a real blood-and-guts kind of guy. "I'm too squeamish for horror," he told Michael Krantz of *Time*. "I can't handle all the blood."

However, he *is* a terror-and-suspense kind of guy, and he says the first film that really made a difference in his life was Steven

Spielberg's *Jaws*. "I'd read the book first, but I was still terrified," he admits. "I sat in the front row and my neck hurt so much that I kept turning my head around, and what I saw was really amazing — a theater full of people, totally involved, screaming in terror. I knew it was what I wanted to do with my life."

From *Jaws*, Williamson gleaned a fundamental truth about young audiences. "Kids like being scared, because when you're a kid, everything is high and low, hot and cold — it's hard to find any calm or middle ground. So a scary movie is a great release for all that pent-up tension and sexual insecurity. For two hours, you can let yourself go. It's relaxing, like having a two-hour therapy session. For me, what connects my stories isn't the scary stuff, but writing about what kids talk about."

As for whether or not movies can still scare him, Kevin says, "Well, I don't get nightmares, but I really get scared. I have to check the closets and look under the bed and in the shower stall all the time. Even to this day when I go home, I have to do it, just because I'm a big scaredy-cat."

In Williamson's scary movie, a deranged killer is slice'n'dicing high-school students. Common enough. But what set the movie apart was the response from the would-be victims. Instead of shrieking in confused horror, they used knowledge absorbed from a vault of bad horror movies. "The biggest mistake you can make is underestimating kids," Williamson tells *USA Today*. "I try to write smart, sophisticated characters who happen to be fifteen."

"Teens today have been exposed to so much," concurs Bob Weinstein, co-founder of Miramax, the company that produced *Scream*. "Writers that don't pander win the game. Kevin understands this brilliantly, and he's got the talent to go with it."

All he knew, Williamson told *Time*, is that he sees today's teen as "a very self-aware, pop-culture-referenced individual who grew up next to Blockbuster in the self-help, psychobabble '80s." And, as such, to Williamson, Neve Campbell was the perfect actress to top-line his film, because "she's very approachable and open, but beautiful and sexy — she's the girl next door and not the girl next door; she's desirable both to girls who like her and guys who want her."

However, despite his after-the-fact devotion to Campbell, she wasn't given the role immediately. "I did two auditions and then I did a screen test," Neve recalls. "It was down to two people. I always have a hard time just being cast in something without auditioning, only because I love the concept of auditioning — of going in and having the challenge of being able to impress and win the role."

Campbell's take on the movie's characters was tinged with hues from her own life experience. "These characters have all grown up with the media, and I don't think any of them had a safe upbringing. Young people have been numbed," she says. "Kevin has a way of capturing that cynicism without being naive."

Campbell says that when she read the script, "It was one of those scripts where I literally couldn't put it down. I found the script extremely intriguing and witty. And I liked the fact that my character, Sidney Prescott, goes from being somewhat of a victim in the beginning of the film, to becoming much stronger and empowered by the end of the film.

"I think, with horror films, the director has to be very cautious and find actors that are going to be able to play the characters in a realistic way so that the film doesn't become a B movie. In a scary film, you're already dealing with extreme circumstances; if it's not played in a realistic way, with some kind of heart, then the film is going to end up being bad quality."

Cathy Konrad, who was a producer on *Scream*, admitted there were some actresses who weren't interested in auditioning because the movie "had the stigma of being a horror movie. It prevented us from getting to a lot of actresses with a brand name for roles," Konrad recalls. "A lot of agents didn't want to put their actresses in, quote, *that kind of movie*. So we looked at a lot of new, fresh faces, and we came in contact with Neve. She's incredibly soulful; there's a lot going on below the surface."

If Neve had any reservations about *Scream*, it was only because she didn't want to be suddenly typecast as the horror princess.

"That was definitely a big concern of mine even taking *Scream*, because I'd done *The Craft*," she acknowledges. "But on the other hand, *Scream* plays a different angle in the genre."

Adding to the panache and hip factor of *Scream* were cameo appearances by some of Hollywood's brightest young stars — Drew Barrymore, for example, enjoyed the notoriety of being the first *Scream* victim. As the killer closes in, he tells her she will survive only if she correctly answers a horror pop quiz: *Who was the killer in the original Friday the 13th movie?* When she incorrectly answers "Jason" (it was his mother — Jason doesn't appear until the sequel), she goes to Ginsu heaven.

For Barrymore, the bloodletting was a blast. According to Drew, she was originally offered the lead role of Sidney Prescott but turned it down, saying she "wanted to be Janet Leigh. Even though she dies so early in *Psycho*, that's who audiences remember, not the sister or boyfriend who try to solve the murder." The role of Sidney Prescott ultimately went to Neve, and perhaps had Barrymore known the life *Scream* would take on, she might have reconsidered her decision. But Drew's loss would be Neve's gain.

As most screenwriters will attest, as fine a script as they might write, a film's success depends on the director. While television is first and foremost a writers' medium, film is all about the director. And in this case, Williamson could not have turned his script over to more in-tune hands than those of horror-meister Wes Craven, whose impeccable credentials included the original *A Nightmare on Elm Street*, plus *The People Under the Stairs*, *Shocker*, *Swamp Thing*, and the seminal genre films *Last House on the Left* and *The Hills Have Eyes*, both of which he wrote, directed, and edited.

Like Williamson's, Craven's background was decidedly unscary. He was born in Cleveland, Ohio, attended Wheaton College in Illinois, and earned a Master's degree in writing and philosophy from John Hopkins University in Baltimore. His film career came relatively late in life, after he had experienced a number of other jobs, including working as a college humanities professor and doing a stint as a New York cabbie. Like Williamson, Craven injected humor in otherwise grisly situations, which kept audiences both screaming and laughing, sometimes simultaneously.

Ironically, though, Craven had begun to move away from horror to other kinds of films when he was sent the *Scream* script. Immediately, its unique approach struck him. "To tell you the truth, I don't watch that many horror movies because I haven't found a lot of good ones," he says in an interview with the *Minneapolis Star Tribune*'s Jeff Strickler. "Most horror films are unrealistic and copycat. They don't inspire you to be a better human being. And I think that's possible by looking into the spiritual elements of fear. Horror movies are about the horror of being mortal. Our well-being — or lack of well-being — depends entirely on a fragile bag of bones. The reason the knife is so often the instrument of destruction in horror movies is that its purpose is to open that bag of bones."

To Craven, *Scream* went beyond simple scares, because to solve the mystery of who the killer was, Sidney Prescott was forced to unearth troubling truths about her family past. "It's really a study of naïveté," he says. "It's really more of a thriller whodunit than a straight horror film."

That more-than-just-a-horror-film element of the script is also what attracted Neve to the role. "I loved the fact that it makes fun of the horror genre within the film," she explains. "People have been saying they love the fact that it's just as funny as it is scary. So, people who wouldn't normally get to a horror film are surprised and enjoy it. And I love the character also, Sidney, who has a big transition in the film. She goes from lost soul to someone who fights back."

Sidney is also someone who got splattered more than a butcher. "I actually had a quote on set where I would say, 'So what am I doing today — screaming, bleeding, crying, or running?' It seems to be what I was doing through the whole film! But on the other hand Sidney was going through a lot of torment and losing a lot of people she loved, so it wasn't hard to get to that place."

One thing Campbell didn't love was her wardrobe in the waning days of the *Scream* shoot, which she describes as "a nightmare, because I was constantly getting slashed at certain points in the movie, or people were getting slashed in front of me and we'd have to have continuity of other people's blood on me. It got a little ridiculous. You pretty much have three or four people attacking you with blood daily, which is a pretty interesting experience. I've done some pretty bloody stuff on Halloween, but I've never been that bloody.

"Because they wanted to keep the continuity on the wardrobe," continues Neve, "they stopped washing it. So, for the last three weeks of shooting the last scene of the movie, I would go in and put on the clothes, and they'd be like cardboard. They'd be so hard, and they'd wet them down again with water and add some more blood." Finally, Campbell exacted her own revenge. "On the last day, I took a paintbrush of blood to a lot of people on the crew, to get back at everyone," she recalls with more than a little satisfaction.

Actually, though, one of the most uncomfortable moments of the film had nothing to do with special effects — it was when Neve had to say the line "With my luck, Tori Spelling will play me in a movie-of-the-week." "I begged director Wes Craven to change the line," Campbell says, grimacing. And for a while, Neve thought he had agreed — he had her say the line replacing Spelling with the talking pig Babe. Then Craven asked her to say the line as written just once "to show the studio we're shooting the script," Campbell says. Naturally, that's the take that made it into the film.

Neve says what she really wanted to do was use her own name instead of Tori's. "I wanted to! I thought that would be actually more intelligent because of the comparison between television and movie stars. They always said that people couldn't do crossover, and I had, so I thought that would be sort of funny."

Audiences uniformly howled at the line, which not only left Campbell wincing, but Spelling wasn't overly amused, either. "I auditioned for Neve's part, so I knew it was in there," she tells Dennis Hensley in *Cosmopolitan*. "The only thing that bothered me was when I was in the theater and I heard people laugh at the line."

It had never been Neve's intention to be disrespectful or hurtful toward anyone, and even though she had no control over the line, she still felt somewhat responsible because she was the one uttering the words on-screen. It weighed on her mind so much, she actually wrote Spelling a letter, but before she'd sent it, she ran into Tori at an audition. "I said that I felt really bad about it and that she really didn't deserve the kind of treatment that she's gotten from the press. It was hard, because we'd been acquaintances before the film and she's always been a sweetheart to me. But she was great when I apologized. She was like 'No, it's O.K. It's just the business.'"

Compared to that emotional trauma, the physical trials of *Scream* seemed easy. "I am very athletic so I love all of the physical stuff I got to do for both *The Craft* and *Scream*," Neve says, adding that the physical demands were part of the fun of doing a horror film. "I love doing action. You know, it's funny, before I did *Scream*, I had said, 'Oh, I'll never do an action film,' because a lot of times there's not a lot of depth to the characters. But after I did *Scream* I was really psyched about being able to fight and punch and do stunt work. I think a lot of that comes from being physically active, because I'm a dancer, so anything physical on a set that's challenging is a lot of fun for me, and that's what I enjoyed."

For the most part, filming *Scream* wasn't a particularly frightening affair, although Neve does allow, "I was obviously aware most of the time that I was in the midst of sixty crew members and a cast and a script, but yes, there are moments when you let your imagination run away with you." Courteney Cox, best known as Monica on *Friends*, once again showed her range as the buttinsky tabloid reporter. "I was in the movie and I still can't watch *Scream* all the way through," Cox admits.

Interestingly, the film's signature image — the hooded black-shroud-donning killer wearing the melting white face mask — came about through sheer serendipity. "We had a lot of problems," acknowledges director Craven. "In Kevin's script, all we had were the words *masked killer*. So we basically had to devise the costume as we were shooting. We didn't even have a satisfactory mask until two days into filming, when we discovered the one we used and quickly bought the rights to it. We also had this big political ruckus in the town we were originally going to shoot in, so we had to go elsewhere."

But once settled, the cast and crew quickly got to work filming. After the opening sequence, during which Drew Barrymore's character, Casey, is telephonically stalked then gutted by the killer, the audience is introduced to Sidney, who lives alone with her dad and her boyfriend, Billy Loomis, played by Skeet Ulrich. Billy is frustrated because Sidney keeps putting off sexual intimacy, perhaps because her mother had been brutally raped and murdered a year earlier. On the strength of Sidney's testimony, Cotton Weary had been convicted of the murder, although a tabloid TV reporter, Gale Weathers, played by Courteney Cox, believes Sidney fingered the wrong man. A day before the anniversary of her mother's killing, Sidney — who is left home alone when her father goes out of town on business — is attacked in her home by the same killer who carved up Casey and her boyfriend Steve. As the death toll mounts, Sidney becomes convinced the murders are connected in some way to her mother, and nearly everyone seems to be a suspect, including her own father.

However, in the end it turns out there's not one killer but two — Billy Loomis and his partner in murderous crime, Stu. Seems Billy went off the deep end when his parents broke up after his mother discovered Billy's father was having an affair with Sidney's mother, who — to Sidney's shocked dismay — was the town harlot. Stu, on the other hand, just joined in for the fun of it. And together they framed Cotton Weary for Mrs. Prescott's murder and made Sidney an unwitting accomplice by ensuring she would misidentify Cotton as the man seen leaving the Prescott home the night of the rape and murder.

However, the butcher boys didn't count on Sidney being quite so tough, and in the film's final scenes she transforms from a frightened victim to an avenger — with some well-timed help from Gale Weathers, who proves handy with a gun.

Neve at the 11th Nancy Susan Reynolds Media Awards, 1995

FITZROY BARRETT / GLOBE PHOTOS

What makes *Scream* so effective, besides the top-notch screenplay and directing, is the quality of the acting, normally so schlocky in slasher films. In addition to Campbell, Cox, and Barrymore, the supporting cast included such up-and-comers as Matthew Lillard and Skeet Ulrich, who has the dubious honor of being constantly compared to Johnny Depp because of their separated-at-birth looks.

As a kid, Ulrich was a nonconformist. "I used to pretend I was like John Denver, of all people, and play the guitar and sing 'Take Me Home, Country Roads,'" he says. Perhaps that's why Ulrich notes, "I didn't have one date in high school. I didn't even go to my prom." He almost didn't go to college, either, after scoring a low 910 on his SAT exams, national tests colleges use to rank potential students. "I didn't care about education. I don't know what I cared about."

Ulrich's home life has also been rocky. His parents divorced when he was young and he's had an on-again, off-again relationship with his father, with whom he once reconciled after tracking him down using the Internet. His relationship with his brother and his mother, who has been married several times, is not much closer.

After losing out on a sports scholarship for college, Skeet enrolled at the University of Carolina in Wilmington and studied marine biology. While there, he began dabbling in acting, doing some extra work, including bit parts in *Chattahoochee* and *Teenage Mutant Ninja Turtles*, where, he says, "I got to beat up the leading lady at the beginning."

Once bitten, Ulrich was hooked. He enrolled in some theater classes and appeared in productions of *The Diary of Anne Frank* and *Hedda Gabler*. Convinced he had found his true calling, Skeet switched his major to theater. When he was twenty-one, he left North Carolina and moved to New York, where he attended New York University and studied with playwright David Mamet and actor William H. Macy at the Atlantic Theater Company.

However, for a while it appeared Skeet might end up being a would-be actor, when his part-time carpentry job started to become a full-time career. "I was remodeling this kitchen for this woman, drawing plans, making estimates. It was going be an eight-month job, and I realized, 'I don't want to be doing this in eight months!'" It was then that the drama gods smiled on Skeet. He was cast in an afterschool special, *Same Difference*, about a Catholic boy in love with a Jewish girl, after which the director, Stacy Cochran, cast him in her 1996 film *Boys*, giving his career the jump start it needed.

Skeet co-starred with Neve in *The Craft* prior to being reunited with her in *Scream* as her boyfriend. Unlike Campbell, who shies away from watching horror films, Skeet loved the genre as a kid. "I remember a friend of mine rolling around in the popcorn on the floor, he was so scared. That's the kind of reaction you like to see. It was so great to get to work with Wes because of how interesting it was watching these films. But I wasn't a *Fangoria* regular. I didn't know what to expect when I first met Wes. I didn't know what he'd look like or how he'd be. The more I talked to him, the more I was fascinated and impressed by how smart he is. When you think of Wes Craven, you don't think *actor's director*, but he really is."

Although he still looks young enough to play a high-school student, Ulrich is a married man these days, having wed actress Georgina Cates in October 1997. "We met two years ago at the *Vanity Fair* Oscar party," Skeet tells Jeanne Wolf in a *YM Magazine* interview. "Georgina introduced herself to me, and the second I looked into her eyes I knew I was going to marry her. I thought, 'Where have you been? I've needed to talk to you forever.'"

Finally having found the familial emotional stability he didn't have as a child, Skeet seems fully grounded and prepared to handle the success coming his way.

Although Matthew Lillard, who plays *Scream*'s second killer, Stu, hasn't garnered the same heartthrob attention that has followed Ulrich, he is highly regarded within the industry as a young actor to watch. Again proving that Hollywood really is just a small industry town, Lillard's co-star in the critically acclaimed film *SLC Punk* was none other than Michael Goorjian, Neve's second-season *Party of Five* boyfriend.

Matthew Lillard was born in Lansing, Michigan, in 1970 but his family moved several times before finally settling in the community of Tustin, California, an hour outside of Los Angeles, which is where Matthew spent his formative years. Short and pudgy as a youth, the now-six-foot-three Lillard was the class clown at Foothill High School. He loved both soccer and acting, and had his first taste of applause in the eighth grade, playing the villain in a speech-class presentation of *Greed for Gold*. He says that was when he realized acting was for him. Plus, as he was teased for being short and chubby, it was a way of stepping out of his own shoes for a while.

The summer after he graduated from high school, Lillard worked as an extra on the film *Ghoulies 3: Ghoulies Go to College*; he was listed as "Matthew Lyn" in the credits. While *Ghoulies 3* might not have been a career stepping stone, he did walk away with his Screen Actor's Guild card and an agent. Matthew says he tried a couple of times to go the traditional college route but realized it simply wasn't for him. "It wasn't my forte," he told Anna Richardson on London television's *The Big Show*.

Acting appealed to Lillard because so many other things didn't. "I wanted to be an actor because it was the only thing I was ever really good at. When you grow up there's the jock clique, the good-looking clique, the geeky clique, and I never really fit into any of those," he says. "The only thing I could do was make people laugh, and when I got into acting it was the only place I could make people laugh and not get kicked out of class for being a smart-ass. It was also the only place when adults actually gave me encouragement. They actually said to a kid that you're good. It's amazing what can happen when you say to someone that doesn't have a lot of confidence, 'Hey — you're good.' And so that just kept me going, kept me going, kept me going, and I just kept achieving at the next highest level."

And some midrange levels, too. Lillard recalls that one of his earliest jobs, as the host of the Nickelodeon series *SK8 TV*, was one of those growing-pains kind of experiences. "It was a skateboarding show, made by skaters for skaters," he recalls. "So I used to have to maintain conversations with skaters: 'So, when did you get into skateboarding?' 'When I was five.' Where do you go from there, as they spit over the camera?"

To better follow his muse, Lillard briefly attended the American Academy of Dramatic Arts in Pasadena, California, and shortly thereafter started his own theater company called the Mean Street Ensemble. "The basic principle," Lillard explains, "was to pay us kids fifty bucks a month — we maintained the theatre space twenty-four hours a day. We did fifteen shows in a year and half. And that was the best thing that I ever did in my life, because I really wanted to do plays in Hollywood. And that's what we did — we were artistic directors at twenty-one, me and my best friend. And you know — we ran around, we had sex and partied and did art — like did plays in the middle of Los Angeles. This was like the best time ever growing up."

Good times aside, Lillard eventually relocated to New York to attend the prestigious Circle in the Square Theatrical School. Although he was driven, the decision wasn't without consequence. "I had to say goodbye to my family when I ran off to New York on my own. I didn't know a soul. That hurt." But it gave Matthew an opportunity to be on his own and mature as both a person and an artist. He appeared in some off-Broadway productions, including *G.O.D.* and *A Child's Christmas in Wales*, eventually getting his first big break in 1994 when he was cast in cult director John Waters's much-touted *Serial Mom*, starring Kathleen Turner as a psychotic Donna Reed type. Although the movie didn't live up to box-office expectations, it was the jump start Matthew needed. He moved back to Los Angeles and appeared in *Mad Love* with Drew Barrymore and *Hackers*, prior to being cast in *Scream*.

Not too surprisingly, *Scream* wouldn't be the last film in which Lillard would play the villain. "Psychos are so much more fun to play, that I just get into them and have a blast," he told *Empire* magazine. "I have the best time and people buy me as a psycho. But I argue that there must be a wee bit of the psycho in everyone out there. I think that everyone has those dreams, those delusions, those ideas of 'Oh, I'd love to kill him — I hate him.' I just get paid to play in them." But, he points out, it's not easy being mean. "You don't want to come across as an idiot. You want to come across as a strong psycho, not some cheesy killer. It takes a lot of energy."

Whether or not he plays on the edge off-camera, Lillard has earned a reputation as an actor not afraid of going *big* on-screen. As Stu in *Scream*, he was a bundle of snapping synapses, a human sparking electrical outlet. "A lot of that at the end of *Scream* wasn't written," Lillard reveals. "It came out of the improv that was all energy!" Of course, sometimes, as Lillard is the first to acknowledge, bigger isn't better for a particular scenario, which he discovered when hired to work on the series *Cybill*. "I was on the set for like three days, and before I ever did a show, they fired me. It was the most horrifying professional experience of my life," he says. But, upon reflection, Matthew admits, "I don't think I was very good at it. I look back now, and go, 'Well, I might have fired me, too.'"

But in the case of *Scream*, Lillard's cinematic eccentricities worked to perfection. "Originally I went in to read for Billy," Lillard told *Time Out New York*. "But they said, 'Well, you're not right for Billy. You're definitely not Skeet Ulrich enough,'" referring to his not-exactly-teen-idol looks. So he was then asked to audition for the role of Deputy Dewey, which would ultimately be played by David Arquette. But Matthew had another part in mind. He told them, "Actually, I'm interested in this kid Stu."

Looking back at the experience now, Lillard considers his association with *Scream* "like being part of a legend." It has been an ongoing boon to his career. Since *Scream*, Lillard has continued to work steadily in a variety of films, including *Wing Commander*, *The Curve*, SLC *Punk*, *She's All That*, *Without Limits*, and Kenneth Branagh's *Love's Labour's Lost*. But when asked if he would like the kind of personal success Neve enjoys and be known as a bona-fide Hollywood star, Lillard is adamant. "No, no, no, I don't want to be a big Hollywood star. I did not get into the business of acting to become rich, powerful, and glamorous. It's not why I'm doing what I do. My ambition that I want to see happen is that I want to take creative control of my career," says Lillard, who has plans to produce as well as direct films in the future. "What you want to do is maintain a healthy artistic career as well as a healthy commercial career. I want to maintain a career that lasts longer than my twenties, and I think I'll be around for a long time."

Scream took about three months to film, which meant Neve went straight from wrapping the movie back to *Party of Five*. She was also doing publicity for *The Craft*. Although she was young and in excellent condition, the work had left her drained. "I'm tired," Campbell admitted at the time. "But it's necessary to get my face out there."

Back on the set of her television show, there was some mild surprise over Neve's decision to take on *Scream*. "It's funny — I wouldn't have suggested that career move, but Neve has made some interesting choices," commented Amy Lippman. "She's been shrewd. If you look at it on the page, the move from a quality drama to a horror film doesn't seem to be a move you'd want to make, but she carefully considered it, and it obviously was a great move for her."

Director Wes Craven agrees with that assessment in an *L.A. Times* interview with David Kronke. "She was on it pretty fast, like a goose on a June bug," Craven says. "She wanted to play something different. She's been a dancer all her life, so she was able to be very physical and was able to control her body within the frame in a way that's quite unique. And from what I've seen on *Party of Five*, that show can be pretty lachrymose, and since this required a lot of crying, she had superb control of that."

Scream was originally scheduled as a spring 1997 release, but the brain trust at Miramax decided to do the movie equivalent of counterprogramming and released their horror film during the Christmas movie season in 1996. Wes Craven thought the idea was folly. "I misunderstood — I thought they said they were releasing it during the *Halloween* season, not the *holiday* season." Despite his skepticism, Craven was willing to take a wait-and-see attitude, understanding that "with the number of movies being released these days, it no longer matters when you come out. You always will have a lot of stuff against you."

The first batch of reviews was decidedly mixed. Beth Pinsker of the *Dallas Morning News* almost audibly sighed, "Sooner or later, Wes Craven is going to have to stop directing horror flicks. He's obviously bored with it. *Scream* is another in his new genre of self-referential and self-deprecating spoofs, following on the heels of 1994's *Wes Craven's New Nightmare*. It's a horror film about how silly horror films are. Wink, wink, nudge, nudge. But how far can he go making fun of his own work?"

What seemed to bother Pinsker and other critics was the response the teens in the movie had to the killing of Barrymore and her boyfriend in the film's opening sequence. As news of the killing spreads, her classmates come to school dressed in the killer's creepy costume — a black hood and a mask fashioned after the face in Edvard Munch's famous painting *The Scream*. And after Neve's character, Sidney, is attacked and the school is closed, the local video store is overrun by kids looking to rent horror films for scare parties.

Other critics, however, appreciated the sharp parody. Jack Garner of Gannett News Service noted, "The teenage slasher film is such a limited, shortsighted formula that any attempt to expand it has to be considered a plus. And veteran horror meister Wes Craven does just that in *Scream*, his new fright-night bloodbath."

Kevin Thomas wrote in *Newsday*, "There's something about Wes Craven's sensational *Scream* popping up in a thicket of year-end prestige releases and holiday pictures that's as subversive as the movie itself. It's sensational in both senses of the word: a bravura, provocative send-up of horror pictures that's also scary and gruesome.

"Although the film has alphabetical billing, its star is Neve Campbell."

On its opening weekend, *Scream* did a respectable $6.3 million. But as word of mouth about the film grew, so did the box office — and the repeat viewers. And like the Energizer Bunny, *Scream* just kept going and going and going. "Normally it's four weekends and you're gone," Miramax honcho Bob Weinstein notes. "But this one stuck around for twenty-six weeks in wide release. It was almost frightening."

Craven was as surprised as the critics who had panned the movie. "We went off to Christmas vacation thinking Beavis and Butt-head had kicked our butts," the director said at the time. "We come back and *Scream* is all people are talking about."

Unlike the box-office profile of most films that peak in the first two weeks, then dramatically drop, *Scream* gained box-office punch, earning $9 million the second week and $10 million by the third. When the dust would finally settle, the film would gross over $100 million domestically and $160 million worldwide. Neve Campbell had the distinction of starring in Miramax's most financially successful movie ever.

While she had hoped the movie would fare well, Neve admitted in an interview with *Australian TV Hits* that she "wasn't always sure how it would be received at the time. It seems that everyone was sort of looking for a horror film, so it was definitely a surprise."

Asked why exactly *Scream* had torn up the box office, Campbell kept it simple. "There just hadn't been any good scary movies in a long time. It makes fun of itself. I also loved the script. But," she added assuredly, "I really don't intend to do too many more in this genre."

Neve had obviously yet to learn the old Hollywood maxim: *Never say never.*

7 Neve Celebrity

During the 1996–1997 television season, *Party of Five*'s third year on the air, the drama truly hit its stride. Ironically, despite all the other awards bestowed on the series, when the Emmy nominations for the 1995–1996 season had been handed out in September 1996, *Party of Five* was completely shut out of the acting and best drama categories. While the omission seemed glaring, those involved in the show took consolation in the fact that their show continued to improve in numbers and quality. When the third season premiered on Fox in August, a month earlier than the other networks' new shows, it was welcomed back with open critical arms.

One of the show's most ardent supporters, USA *Today* critic Matt Roush, wrote a review tantamount to love poetry: "Suffice it to say none of this premature activity measures up to the return of *Party of Five*, that rare youth-appeal drama with heart and soul as well as a sex drive. With its poignant story lines beautifully played by a poster-perfect cast that would look at home on any dorm wall, this show enjoys an unusual alchemy that transforms soap-opera contrivances into deeply felt quality drama."

Mike Hughes of Gannett News Service offered a more backhanded compliment. "Life will *never* be easy for the Salinger kids. They think too much, talk too much, worry too much. If they don't, someone will do it for them. Still, we keep watching *Party of Five* because . . . well, because it's better than shows where characters don't think at all.

"This is an earnest show that works hard. Despite all those pretty faces, it hires only people with genuine acting talent. *Party of Five* moves us often and amuses us occasionally. Afterward, we appreciate the pleasures of any unexamined moment."

However, whatever angst some critics still felt, the atmosphere on the set of *Party of Five* was relaxed. "It's not like we're sitting on our laurels and kicking back, but now we don't have to constantly prove ourselves week after week," explained Matthew Fox to Matt Roush.

For producers Lippman and Keyser, the third season meant an opportunity to concentrate more on writing and worry less about whether the show would survive another week. "The first year was about not getting canceled," recited Amy Lippman. "The second year was about trying to build an audience, and our reward was not having to sweat out a pickup this year. We don't need to rush to that taped phone message that gives you ratings every Thursday morning."

Having lasted into a third season, the show's creators actually found their dramatic well more full than when they started. "One of the advantages we have with this group of characters who are actually getting older is they're always hitting new milestones," said Chris Keyser. "There's no problem in coming up with a whole new set of interesting complications for them. This means characters will begin to exhibit traits that are not the same as you've seen before."

Lippman picked up the dramatic line of thought from her partner. "We get a lot of story mileage out of a character making a mistake and actually regretting it," the producer said. "What's interesting this season is he begins to deal with that character flaw: What does it mean to love someone, and what does it mean to be there for them in a crisis?"

Lippman wanted the third season to be one in which Neve's character, Julia, would try to decide what kind of future she wanted. Of course, she would still be dealing with her decision to dump Justin in favor of the-boy-your-father-warns-you-about Griffin, but primarily the producers wanted Julia to have a *real* choice to make. "We've always played her as a real student who has very high expectations for herself and every intention to go off to school and become a writer," Lippman said. "Over the season, we'll challenge her assumptions."

Of course, this kind of detailed, thought-out story-writing meant eighteen-hour days and few weekends to relax at home, but Keyser and Lippman appeared glad to make the sacrifice. "It has always been our contention people won't tune in based on the lines in *TV Guide*," Lippman explains. "They really have to care about the characters on a weekly basis. We ourselves are less interested in the stories that spin each character out to lots of different relationships. They always need to come home to the sense of family — what do we mean to each other, how do we help each other — and hopefully not in a saccharine way.

"These kids are constantly disappointing each other, which means you don't always end the show with everyone hugging and crying and saying how much they love each other. Sometimes family members hurt each other. And I think an audience's investment in what this family means to each other is what is going to keep us on the air."

Campbell assessed her character at the beginning of the third season this way: "Julia is slightly confused. Considering what she went through last year with the miscarriage, she's not in the right frame of mind to be sexually active. She's dealing with that in the beginning of the season, and deciding to refrain from being sexual and trying to find a different way of having love. Also, I think this season is more about what she wants in life, and becoming more clear about whether she wants to know now what it is that she wants to be, or whether she's going to relax a bit and take some time to enjoy her life and grow."

Perhaps the biggest difference between the start of the third season and its conclusion in the spring of 1997 was that suddenly the dynamics of celebrity among the cast members had changed. Instead of all the attention being focused on Scott Wolf and Matthew Fox, the one-two punch of *The Craft* and *Scream* had propelled Julia to the head of the Salinger clan. Suddenly, fans and the media couldn't get enough of their newly crowned ingénue princess. But showing that she wasn't going to go all blockbuster Hollywood, Neve continued to participate in projects that had little commercial appeal, simply because the subject was of interest to her, such as *Twisted Love: Dating Violence Exposed*.

Although the title smacked of afternoon talk-show titillation, the program, which aired on PBS, was a serious look at difficult subjects seldom discussed, such as dating abuse, when a partner is either physically, emotionally, or verbally assaulted. Campbell served as one of the guest hosts for the show, which offered case studies as well as options viewers could avail themselves of.

However, while Neve could feel good about using her growing celebrity for a social service such as that, most of the time she found herself struggling to adapt to the intense pressure of being constantly scrutinized and sought after. "It's kind of difficult to be oblivious to the attention. It may be a sign of success, but I don't get off on fame at all."

In fact, Neve admitted to *Entertainment Weekly*, it can be positively annoying at times. "There's nowhere I can go without being recognized. During private dinners, people will be like, 'Excuse me, I know you hate this, but. . . .' And it's like, 'If you know I hate it, why are you doing it?' That's not part of what I wanted."

Beyond that, as she told *Sassy* magazine, "The hardest thing is that I've had to become more guarded now that I'm in the public eye — and I don't like having to be cautious. I'm considering tinting the windows on my car because I've had people follow me. I'm in people's living rooms every week and so fans think they know me, but the truth is they don't know me. They know Julia, not Neve."

Fame and celebrity not only affect actors themselves but also all the people in their lives, particularly spouses, who find it disconcerting and often infuriating to be constantly interrupted by strangers when in public. But Campbell said she was lucky because Jeff was "fine with it. He's very happy for me, very supportive."

Colt tried to show good humor by making a joke of some of the more awkward moments. "People call me Mr. Campbell," Colt said in *People* magazine. He also admitted he wasn't thrilled with Neve's ongoing love scenes with her on-screen boyfriends. But keeping it light, he added he only worried "when she calls out 'Justin' in the middle of the night."

While Colt seemed to dwell on perceived trespasses on his position in Neve's life, Campbell was more worried about how celebrity might affect her as a person. "I don't want to put up barriers," she reiterated to the *New York Post*, "but I find myself in circumstances where some people want to be your friend because of who you are, instead of who you are inside. It's hard to believe that a job can cause that to happen, but it does."

And the idea that some people might only be drawn to her because of some perceived image disturbed Campbell. "I think my greatest insecurity would just be standing in the middle of the room and having everyone watching me think that's what I want," she told *TV Guide*. "If I am interesting to you because of who I am, then that's incredible. But if I'm interesting to you only because of what I am, then let's not bother, you know?"

Then there was the matter of suddenly finding herself in the position of role model. "People always ask, 'What's it like to be looked up to by teens?' It's a wonderful position to be in. It's wonderful that people look up to me and that they can learn things from Julia. I acknowledge that I have this huge impact on teenage girls and I try to be aware of the things that are going on within my character," she notes. While she admits that it's "wonderful to be playing a female character that so many girls can look up to," at the same time she doesn't "want to steer girls in the wrong direction.

"I am an actor first. I didn't choose to be a politician. I didn't ask people to follow all my steps. That's not what I'm saying. I am trying to entertain people. And I think it's a parent's responsibility to watch what their children are watching. It's not really my responsibility. I'm an artist. It's like, where's the line? I'm a human being and I'm Neve before I'm anything else. And I'm not going to pretend to be anything I don't want to. This business takes up so much of your life as it is that you shouldn't give up yourself," Campbell say. Then she adds, "But on the other hand, I'm an actress and scripts are handed to me and it's up to me to choose what's a responsible script to take and what is not. So, it's like trying to find a balance between both of those things."

Even though Campbell complained about the need to be cautious, she was still surprisingly candid, both about work and life. While making the publicity rounds for *The Craft*, Neve waxed nostalgic about the experience, but later on she let down her guard a bit. "The truth is, I didn't want to do the film at all because I was really tired," she says. "I also wasn't in the mood to work with other girls my own age because I was afraid it would become catty or competitive. But the character intrigued me. She goes from being this freak burn victim, who doesn't fit in at all, to this beautiful girl when she removes her scars through witchcraft." And when asked if her fears of competition on the set were unfounded, Campbell stops herself. "Let's just say that because of the hours and because it's such a dark film, it was a really odd experience."

And she was just as unexpectedly honest about herself, too, when she engaged one reporter about her body. "My eyes are too close together and I have funny-looking knees, but my feet are the worst," she offered. "I have terrible bunions from all that dancing — really horrible. I have arthritis in my toes and I'm in pain a lot, so I'm having surgery on them after my next movie. My toes are really ugly, really enormous. And they're hairy, too. You know, a lot of people have hairy toes but just won't admit it. But because my toes are so much bigger, it's very obvious," she said. "I'm not vain, so it doesn't bother me that much that I have hairy toes."

And if that wasn't enough, Neve let out another secret. "I'm pretty disorganized. Actually I'm a pig. I'm so messy. I leave my clothes all over the place. And I spend so little time at home that the last thing I want to do when I'm in is cleaning. And I hate doing pots and pans. Washing up sucks so badly."

In other words, Neve wasn't a closet glam queen. Instead, she was happy to call herself "the girl next door. I don't walk around in elegant gowns all day. On my days off I lie around in pajamas — my favorite pair have cows all over them."

And when she does go out, Neve admits to liking a drink or two. "I love red wine and vodka and tonic — and beer, because I'm a Canadian. I don't get hangovers very often. I take loads of vitamins and drink loads of water and just get on with it. I'm a happy drunk. I become very open. But I don't drink to the point where I fall over."

That kind of girlfriend dish is exactly what many fans found so appealing about Neve. Producers, on the other hand, saw a steadily improving body of work. "This new wave of talent is all-consuming in Hollywood right now," *Scream* producer Cathy Konrad told *Time*'s Christopher John Farley. "Neve has a step up because audiences have been identifying with her for years on *Party of Five*. When she makes her real star turn, she'll have a body of work behind her."

Uppermost in Neve's mind seemed to be a desire to consciously break away from her teen persona. "I definitely want to play someone my age," Campbell admitted to Canadian *TV Guide* reporter Ellen Vanstone in the summer of 1996, when she was twenty-two years old. "I love the roles, and there's a lot to work with when you're playing a young character because there's a lot of vulnerability. But I don't want to be seen only as Julia or pigeonholed as a sixteen- or seventeen-year-old.

"The truth is," Neve continued, "it can become tedious. But on the other hand, when I play teenagers, there's a lot of depth that comes into the characters with a teenager because of teenage angst. I know when I was a teenager, like so many other teenagers, everything — like a broken nail — is a drama somehow for some reason. There's integrity behind it somehow. So you can actually find a lot of levels to teenagers, because they're going through so much and so much insecurity and so much learning and so much growth."

Campbell seemed aware that her own life and career were developing on a path curiously parallel to Julia's. Every day was a learning experience, as she honed her attitudes about work and life. Although she loved *Party of Five* and considered her co-stars extended family, she also knew that another series was not likely to be in her future. "Being on a series is hard because it takes a lot longer to get through to the end of the season," she explained. "You're aware that you've got nine months to go when you start. And the hours tend to be somewhat longer. Movies I love, because you get to do different characters and eventually that's where I hope to go — strictly feature films. At that point, I'll have more time off, I'll be able to choose my films and characters, and feel somewhat more creative because I'll be able to play different characters."

Because she had worked almost nonstop since arriving in Los Angeles, in some ways Campbell still felt like an out-of-towner in her adopted city. "I'm not very fond of Los Angeles, but I've also been working so much that I haven't really had time to give it a chance," Campbell acknowledged. But she also allowed, "I've met a few people this year who are wonderful and I'm starting to feel more comfortable."

Helping make the City of Angels feel homier was her brother Christian, who had also moved to Los Angeles to pursue his acting career. "It's great having him here," Neve said. "We're very similar. My brother and I are both very focused and we always have been, and determined. My brother's a wonderful, wonderful person. He's probably my best friend in the whole world and we're extremely close. So, I think that's probably why there's a lot of resemblance in our work."

Except having a brother in your own age bracket can cause some curious work encounters, such as when they went for auditions "in which our characters are supposedly love interests!" Neve laughs.

While it's always difficult coming to L.A. and establishing a career, it can be doubly frustrating if you are chasing someone else's shadow. But Christian Campbell was determined to forge his own path and one of the ways he did that was to co-found a theater company in L.A. called Blue Sphere Alliance, which Neve says he did on his own. "I didn't set it up with him — I haven't got time to run one! He's actually running it, but I'm in the company. He'll do quite well," Neve said of Christian. "He's real talented."

Apparently, acting talent really does run in the family because their younger half-brother, Alex Campbell, got his first series in Canada at age twelve. Christian's first big American break came when he was cast as Teddy Delacourt on the short-lived *Malibu Shores*, described by some critics as *90210* at the beach. Like his sister, Christian claims to have been way outside the in crowd during high school. "I was geeky," he says. "I would watch the cute girls flirt with the guys, but I was never one of those guys."

With Neve usually too busy to travel home to Canada, her family is steadily migrating south. Neve has bought a house for her mom less than a mile from her own in L.A., and they both live a short distance from Christian. And Neve and Christian's other half-brother, Damian MacDonald, who Neve refers to as a computer genius, has also relocated to Southern California, where he works as a Web-site designer. What's particularly close to her heart about Damian is that he suffers from Tourette's syndrome, and Campbell has been very public and vocal about supporting the Tourette Syndrome Association.

But for Neve, during that year of *Party of Five*'s third season there were not enough hours in a day. "I don't have an awful lot of time," she lamented, saying she had to "be very careful of spreading myself too thin right now, because I'm working so much."

Little did she know, but things were about to get a whole lot busier.

ED GELLAR / GLOBE PHOTOS

GREG VIE / GLOBE PHOTOS

CAT RUN PROD INC. / SHOOTING STAR

The cast of *Party of Five*

©PACHA / CORBIS

Neve and her family

LISA ROSE / GLOBE PHOTOS

RUSSELL EINHORN / LIAISON AGENCY

NED REDWAY / GLOBE PHOTOS

RUSSELL EINHORN / LIAISON AGENCY

Neve and her brother Christian

DAVID ROHMER / LIAISON AGENCY

©PACHA / CORBIS

EVAN AGOSTINI / LIAISON AGENCY

Neve and Matthew Lillard at the 1998 Academy Awards

GREGG DEGUIRE / LONDON FEATURES

KEVIN MAZUR / LONDON FEATURES

Neve, David Bowie, and Sarah Michelle Gellar

©PACHA / CORBIS

Courtney Cox, Neve, and Rose McGowan

8 Neve: Riding the Wave

During her *Party of Five* hiatus in the spring of 1997, Neve Campbell was once again off making movies. In mid-April she traveled to the sultry shores of Miami to begin work on an offbeat film called *Wild Things* that was guaranteed to help Neve shed her good-girl-next-door image. Directed by John McNaughton and co-starring Matt Dillon, Denise Richards, and Kevin Bacon, who also served as one of the film's producers, *Wild Things* was an erotic whodunit that truly left the viewers guessing until the credits rolled.

Described by a studio publicist as *Baywatch* meets *Body Heat*, *Wild Things* tells the story of an apparently upstanding south Florida high-school guidance counselor named Sam Lombardo (Dillon) who is accused of rape by one of his students, the rich and very bratty Kelly Van Ryan (Richards), whose mother — as bad luck would have it — is Sam's ex-lover. Neve plays Kelly's white-trash classmate, Suzie Toller, who just happens to have a genius-level IQ. When Suzie also charges Sam with rape, his career is finished and his freedom is at stake. Kevin Bacon co-stars as a local detective who suspects not everything is what it seems, and Bill Murray comes aboard as Sam's ethically impaired lawyer, Ken, who takes the case when nobody else will.

During the rape trial, Sam's affair with Kelly's mother (Theresa Russell) is revealed. Sam is acquitted after Suzie breaks down on the witness stand and admits that Kelly put her up to fabricating a story of Sam's raping her, too. Once free, Sam walks away with a multimillion-dollar settlement from Kelly's mother for all his pain and suffering. Then about halfway through the movie, the plot begins to thicken with developments truly too complicated to go into.

As she prepared for the role, Neve made a conscious effort not to think too much beyond the work itself. "I don't feel pressure," she said in an *Australian TV Hits* interview. "I'm just sort of riding the wave right now and allowing my career to go in the direction that it seems to be going. You know, trying to be intelligent about my choices and not just throwing myself into whatever film is offered. Whatever happens, happens."

Her professed philosophy was bolstered by a chance meeting with Robert De Niro, who had worked with *Wild Things* director McNaughton on *Mad Dog and Glory*. They shared a table at a Martin Scorsese tribute, and during dinner conversation, Neve mentioned she was nervous about her upcoming role in *Wild Things* "because it was very extreme and very different from what I'd done. He said, 'You know what? You're young. Do the movie. If it's a mistake, you're still young.' And that was pretty great."

What had given Neve clammy palms was her character's wrong-side-of-the-tracks baggage. "I played an ex-convict, a drug-addicted bisexual. That was the challenge, and that's why I took the role, because I wanted to be seen in a different light. I wanted to play someone who was the complete opposite of Julia," she says. "Someone who has a little evil in her. It's really fun doing something you've never done before. I don't think it's what people expect of me, but that's sort of the reason I did it. I want a little longevity in my career. And I want to be able to look back on my career, when I'm fifty years old, and have a huge library of different kinds of characters."

That said, it still can be nerve-wracking to play against comfortable type. "There's definitely apprehensions when you choose to do a film and to do a role that is very different from anything you've ever done," Campbell admitted in an *E! Online* interview. "On the other hand, I wanted to be courageous about that — you know my plan, hopefully, is that I have some longevity in my career and that I play all different kinds of characters. And I keep challenging myself, so for me the fun and the challenge outweigh the apprehension."

Campbell explains it further to Stephanie Sheh of *University Wire*. "The very reason I took this movie is because I got to play the bad girl, because I wanted to challenge myself in that way and learn what it is to play someone evil. For the same reason, I don't want to be typecast as a television actress. I don't want to be typecast as just one kind of character, just a good girl." Plus, Campbell adds, "It's always more fascinating to me to play characters who are really messed up because I'm not really close to those kinds of people in my life. And it's fascinating to try and understand why people choose to go in an evil direction in their lives."

As it happened, Campbell might not even have appeared in *Wild Things* if she hadn't taken the time to give the script a second reading. The first time around, she described the *Wild Things* script as "the worst piece of trash" she had ever read. But once she "got the humor of it, and the absurdity of it," she had to do it.

To play Suzie Toller in the film, Neve did some preshoot research by visiting female inmates in local Miami jails. "I met a young woman and we were supposed to talk about half an hour but we ended up talking for about four hours because we really hit it off," Campbell remembers. "She expressed to me why she made certain decisions in her life and why her life had gone in such a bad way and what the experience was to be in jail." Interestingly, the inmate had no idea who Campbell was.

Meeting with the inmate helped Neve "create a history" for Suzie, a character backstory Neve would use throughout the film. "She has not had a whole lot of respect her entire life," Campbell says of the character. "She also has not had any guidance, and is a girl from the wrong side of the tracks. She hasn't had a lot of good things come to her in her life and thus is very angry."

Perhaps most shocking initially to moviegoers was Suzie's punked-out look — the tattoos and dyed hair. "The look was especially important, because my audience really needs to not see Julia in this performance," Campbell explains. "I wanted to veer away from that. So we punked up my hair, got tattoos, short shorts. The first time they did all that in makeup, I scared myself. I wouldn't want to meet that girl in a dark alley."

Walking around in her alter ego was fun for Neve. "It's kind of an odd experience actually, when you punk yourself out like that. I'd walk into stores in Miami and some people wouldn't recognize me, and they would ignore me or not serve me or watch to see if I was stealing anything. It was really interesting to understand that kind of prejudice. And it made me understand why punks go to even further extremes, because it made me want to do even more."

Although *Wild Things* had a very clever script with twists and turns throughout, the biggest buzz generated prior to the movie's release in May 1998 was over two sex scenes, one of which involved a three-way between Matt Dillon, Denise Richards, and Neve. But those *Party of Five* devotees hoping to catch a glimpse of Campbell in the buff were destined to be disappointed because Campbell had the clout to get a no-nudity clause in her contract.

"I don't think of it as much about clout as about control," Campbell avers. "I want to control my own career. That's how I was brought up: to fight for the control of my own destiny. I come from a family of fighters. If I have to show my breasts, then I shouldn't be doing the movie at all — that's sort of how I feel. But you wouldn't believe the stuff that goes into my contract," she adds, shaking her head. "'No side of breast, no nipple, only down to the small of the back,' and so on. You need to set those boundaries before you get on the set."

Campbell says nudity depends, though, on the circumstances. "For me it's about the characters, and I didn't really feel that it was necessary for this character. I've played another character where she was a real nature child in a film that I did for Europe, and it was a film about her skinny-dipping with an animal in the middle of the forest. It wasn't about graphic sex and about box-office draw, so I was comfortable with that. But when it comes to box-office draw, I don't feel as comfortable with that."

However, lest anyone think Neve is a prude, she stresses, "I don't have anything against actresses who do nude scenes."

In fact, Campbell was very supportive and empathetic with co-star Denise Richards, who didn't have the luxury of a no-nudity clause. Prior to *Wild Things*, Richards was best known for her roles as Loni Anderson's daughter in *Melrose Place* and a spaceship pilot sent to war against giant intergalactic bugs in the gory sci-fi thriller *Starship Troopers*. "A month after I wrapped *Starship*, I read the *Wild Things* script," Richards recalls. "And even though it's a thriller and it's got a lot of twists and a lot of people are evil, I was like, 'I love this!'"

Not willing to leave winning such an intriguing role to chance, Richards called an executive producer to campaign for the part of Kelly Van Ryan, the rich, manipulative high-school girl at the center of the movie's complex plot. The producers had actually been hoping to cast Neve for the part. "They wanted her for my role, but she wanted to play another part, thankfully, or I wouldn't have been in it," Richards says.

Director McNaughton says when Denise came in for her first audition she was good, but "not so good we had to hire her. But when she came back for a second audition, she was a lot better. She'd obviously thought about the character, which we took as a good sign that she could do the role." And being the ever-pragmatic Hollywood director, he added, "If worse came to worst, we knew she'd be beautiful."

Richards, who had not done any film nudity before, notes that *Wild Things* had to be "a very special project for me to do it. They wanted me to do it for *Starship* and I wouldn't, because I felt it wasn't necessary for my character or the story."

Necessary or not, it was still nerve-wracking disrobing with a gaggle of crew members staring on. "I've read stuff where actresses feel very free and, you know, it feels great — I don't think that's the case! It's the most vulnerable position to be in! But I had to get through it. Otherwise they could find someone else."

Helping her get through it were her co-stars, particularly Campbell, who says even though she didn't know Denise prior to filming, working with her on such an intimate level "was fun. It was totally fine. I had no problem with it. We were a little nervous because it was a sex scene and that's always nerve-wracking on a set. But otherwise, no, I didn't have apprehensions about what audiences would think.

"My feeling on sex scenes is that once you commit to doing it, you can't feel uncomfortable about doing it," Neve says. "Audiences will sense that you're uncomfortable, and you can't allow that. So you have to find ways to be comfortable, and that's the reason I drank."

But before indulging in wine, margaritas, and tequila, Campbell says she and Denise "sat down and discussed the scene. I was very sensitive to Denise's situation. She chose to do nudity, and she was very nervous. So we sat down and mapped out our boundaries, how we were going to do the scene. I think it was a touchy scene to do because Denise wasn't extremely comfortable with the nudity. So it was about making her comfortable and talking about her parameters and all her other boundaries, deciding what we were comfortable with and what we weren't comfortable with and being professional about it."

But, as Campbell points out, no amount of discussing can ever eliminate all of the strangeness of the moment. "Honestly, doing any kind of love scene is an awkward experience. I mean, how many jobs are there out there where you're asked to take off your clothes with people who are strangers — an audience or crew — and make out? But I kept telling her not to worry about how they were going to make her look. I told her that it was in their best interest to make her look good."

As for actually kissing a woman — Campbell and Richards have another scene in which they share erotic embraces by themselves — Neve says she "didn't have any kind of trepidation," either with the kiss itself or people's possible reactions to it. "I am completely O.K. with homosexuality, bisexuality, whatever people's sexual choices are," Campbell says. "I would hope people would be more shocked about violence in a movie than about a kiss."

Even so, Campbell fully realized, as she told *Journal Now* reporter

Neve and her *Wild Things* co-stars, Denise Richards and Kevin Bacon

GREGG DEGUIRE / LONDON FEATURES

Roger Moore, "People will definitely be shocked seeing me this way. Certain people are not going to get this. They are going to find it uncomfortable to laugh at things they see. Some of my friends from the Family Film Awards, who just gave me an award, may want to revoke it after seeing this movie," she only half-joked. "But that's the fun of it. As long as you sit down and know that it's about extreme people, that it's all right to laugh at the absurdities you see, then you'll have a good time."

Oh, and yes, Campbell said patiently in one junket interview after another, Denise was a good kisser, and yes, their tongues touched. "Men love to see two women together," Denise Richards told *Entertainment Weekly*'s Benjamin Svetkey. Then she asked, "Why is that? Explain it to me."

But she and Campbell weren't sure what the fuss was all about. "Neve and I saw the film at a special screening, and we were so nervous, we couldn't stop laughing. I'll have to ask my guy friends if it's erotic or not. When you see yourself up there, all you want to do is cringe."

Richards confessed to Svetkey that, "when you think about it, it's kind of a strange job I have. At one point during *Wild Things*, we were shooting at night and I just sat there and thought, 'It's four o'clock in the morning. I'm half-naked in a swimming pool. I'm making out with Neve Campbell. What am I doing here?'"

But Richards is emphatic in her praise of Campbell. "I think she did an amazing job. I think she was very convincing when we were in our scenes and when they said 'Cut' we would laugh."

Had it not been for the focus on the sex scenes, reporters might have paid more attention to some other curious happenings during the shoot, such as the tornado that came terrifyingly close to the location base camp — and the time a dead body floated by during a scene. "Kevin Bacon, Daphne Rubin-Vega, and I were shooting a scene together next to a swamp and all of the sudden one of the crew says, 'Cut!'" recalls Campbell. "And they said there was a dead body in the water. And so the cops came by and were like, 'You making a movie?' And we were like, 'Yeah.' So they actually

— typical Hollywood — held the body next to the dock so it wouldn't float through the shot so we could finish the scene."

Overall, though, the shoot was a good experience for Neve. "Matt Dillon, Kevin Bacon, Bill Murray, you can't beat that," she says. "They're wonderful and talented and inspiring and really down to earth and a lot of fun."

When the movie wrapped, the randy crew gifted Richards with an inscribed silver vibrator while Neve was presented with a pearl necklace.

When *Wild Things* premiered, many wondered if both Richards and Campbell would be requesting masks to disguise themselves from family, friends, and critics. "My parents aren't coming to the premiere. They're not invited," Richards told Janet Weeks of *USA Today*. "They supported my decision to do the film. But I just don't want to see their faces right after they see it." Denise admitted she knew her parents would eventually see the film on their own, "but I don't want my dad to see my breasts. I'm just hoping he'll cover his eyes."

Campbell was equally nervous, but was given support by her mother. "She's an actress and started acting again," says Neve. "She totally understands the process. As I was sinking into the chair for some of the scenes, she'd take my hand and say, 'It's O.K., honey.' She was great."

Even so, tattles brother Christian, Neve was still shy. "I was with her at the *Wild Things* premiere, and I could see her sink into her seat during the make-out scenes," he laughingly told Christopher John Farley of *Time*.

And, for the most part, the critics thought Neve and the film were, while not great, good.

"*Wild Things* is lurid trash," wrote Roger Ebert in the *Chicago Sun-Times*, "with a plot so twisted they're still explaining it during the closing titles. It's like a three-way collision between a soft-core sex film, a soap opera, and a B-grade noir. I liked it. The movie solidifies Neve Campbell's position as the queen of slick exploitation, gives Matt Dillon and Kevin Bacon lots of chances to squint ominously, and has a sex scene with Denise Richards that is either gratuitous or indispensable, depending on your point of view."

"This movie has everything," Ruthe Steine declared in the *San Francisco Chronicle*. "A slyly dopey beginning that places us in the awkward milieu of high school lust, and then a midsection that gives us a tour of our characters' murky pasts. In Stephen Peters' nasty script there is dissembling, sexuality of all flavors, greed, murder, betrayal, and stupidity."

"Campbell and Richards are good, as are Dillon and Bacon," concurred Barbara Schulgasser in the *San Francisco Examiner*. "Russell still can't act, but she is perfect in her ineptitude as a sluttish mother. Robert Wagner, playing a society lawyer and pillar of the community, is my favorite. In scenes with opposing counsel Murray, he looks like he can barely keep from dissolving into tears of laughter."

Richards had more riding on the film's success or failure than Campbell, because she had neither a series to fall back on nor the body of work Campbell had already amassed. "I want to be careful with my choices," she notes. "I want to have a long career. And I just hope people will take me seriously."

That said, some might question her decision to be the most recent Bond girl in that franchise's latest installment, *The World Is Not Enough*. In the film, she plays a nuclear-weapons expert. "Being a Bond girl is not the worst thing that can happen," Richards says. "If it limits what I do in the future, it's my fault, because that's not who I am."

Campbell, too, was still worried about being limited in her film roles, particularly as she prepared to revisit Sidney Prescott in *Scream 2*.

9 Time to Slow Down

Long before *Scream* became the highest-grossing horror movie of all time, plans had been made to film a sequel. In fact, Kevin Williamson's original deal included a full trilogy of films. Then once it blew away previous box-office records, Miramax was more than a little anxious to get the sequel in theaters by December 1997 — just a year after the original was released. That kind of timetable was almost unheard of. But what the Weinsteins wanted, the Weinsteins usually got. Of course, it did cost them a chunk of their film fortune when Williamson negotiated a seven-figure deal with Miramax Films for two sequels as well as a new installment in the *Halloween* horror franchise.

Producer Cathy Konrad tried to explain the rush to David Hochman of *Entertainment Weekly*. "Everybody's looking for something identical to *Scream*. But because we have the brand name, we need to jump in and give the people more of what they want, as long as they continue to want it."

What complicated matters was that screenwriter Williamson had suddenly become one of the hottest commodities in town. In addition to having his script for *Killing Mrs. Tingle* — with which he would make his directorial debut — rescued from obscurity, he had also created a quasi-autobiographical series for the WB, *Dawson's Creek*, that was a most demanding writing mistress. Miramax didn't care — they needed a script and gave Williamson three weeks to deliver. "The Miramax mafia basically came down to North Carolina where we were shooting *Dawson's Creek*," he recalls.

"They came to harass me, and to make sure I wasn't going to eat, sleep, or breathe anything other than the plot of *Scream 2*." Amazingly, Williamson not only finished on time, but came up with a script every bit as good as the original.

Not only did the creative duo of Williamson and Wes Craven want to match the original, they actually sought to perform the rare feat of going one better, something only a handful of films had ever done, most notably *The Godfather Part II*. "A sequel just needs to be approached with respect for the material," director Craven explained to Stephen Applebaum of *The Independent*. "It should involve the same team and ideally the same writer; and it should follow the central protagonist, rather than the villain that you crank out as action figures. A film like *Scream 2*, which follows the development of a woman who had a traumatic series of events in her life two years earlier, is much more interesting to me. And the other part of the film, which is referential to the genre that's its heart, is interesting because it means we can talk about sequels and their homicidal parallel, copycat killers. We're bludgeoned with that whole issue every time we go out and do press, so it's interesting to be able to take that particular bull by the horns in a film."

Craven continued his professorial musings with *Entertainment Weekly*'s Bruce Fretts. "Horror movies deal with the overriding, barely expressed fears of a culture," he observed. "Teenagers are very susceptible to it because they're just coming into an awareness of the world at large. *Who should you trust, who should you be friends with?* They know they're about to become adults and about to have to find a mate and have children and do all those very scary things."

Initially, Neve Campbell admits, she had her own concerns about the sequel, which she was contractually bound to do. "I was worried about being typecast as a *Scream* queen kind of thing. And I had apprehensions because the only reason any sequel is ever made is that the first one was so good. You think, 'Who are we to try and outdo ourselves?' But I was incredibly happy when I read Kevin Williamson's script. I felt it was not as funny — it was funnier — and not as scary — it was scarier — so I was both surprised and elated."

However, Neve showed up for work lacking much excitement — it was a different experience working on the sequel. "I just came off of *Wild Things* and went straight into this, so the enthusiasm of being on a new movie is sort of not there for me. Last year it was like being at summer camp, and this year it's like I've been at summer camp too long and I'd like to go home," she admitted to *Australian TV Week* correspondent Josh Rottenberg.

Because the first *Scream* hit the public without warning, the surprise ending was relatively easy to keep under wraps prior to the film's release. However, because *Scream 2* was so anxiously awaited, the filmmakers knew they needed to go to extraordinary lengths to keep the script's story from leaking out in advance. They realized this after Williamson's initial forty pages quickly found their way onto the Internet. As the screenwriter scrapped all those pages and started over, Craven and the producers began battening down the production hatches, beginning with the auditioning process. "We were trying to cast without a screenplay, with very vague characterizations," recalls producer Konrad. "Scripts, minus a lot of pages, were taken to people's houses. I felt like an idiot. I told people, 'I know this is really silly, but this is what we gotta do.'"

The upside, though, was that "it let people know we cared about keeping the thrill out there for audiences. The fun on the first one was because it was so unexpected. We wanted to try not to let everybody know what happened in this one."

For Craven, it was a whole new experience. But he energetically warmed to the task. A security policy was instituted that required approved visitors to wear badges, and scenes were distributed in installments and filmed out of order. The script was even reproduced on colored paper, "where no one could read it at all. Everyone was saying, 'Can you read this line?'" The production's Achilles' heel, though, was the crowd shots set at movie theaters that necessitated bringing in extras. Craven noted ruefully that the opening scene of *Scream 2*, set in a movie theater, ended up described on the Internet in glorious detail.

So obsessive was the secrecy around the script that even the actors developed a siege mentality. "When I first got the script," says Jerry O'Connell, who plays Campbell's devoted boyfriend, to David Hochman of *Entertainment Weekly*, "two men with Uzis delivered it and stayed with me until I was done reading it." Cast member Jada Pinkett adds that right up until the end of the shoot, "none of us were given the last twenty pages of the script so nobody knew whether they were the killer or not."

Unlike the first installment, when the filmmakers had to beg agents to let their clients read, *Scream 2* became *the* hip movie to snag a role in. "They were breaking down doors to get into the sequel," Craven tells Hochman. One of those who came a-knocking was Sarah Michelle Gellar, better known to her fans as that most empowered of teen females, Buffy the Vampire Slayer. "I so desperately wanted to be a part of this movie," acknowledges Gellar, who says she called her agent and begged for an audition. "It just had a cool feeling about it."

And in a master stroke of casting, Tori Spelling — the butt of so much teasing, thanks to the infamous line in *Scream* — plays Neve's character in *Stab*, the film within the film in *Scream 2*, proving that life has a funny way of evening things out. "Yeah," agrees Spelling. "Without that line, my part wouldn't have been in the second movie, and so, ha-ha, it all worked out."

Interestingly, even though he was old enough to be a father to most of his cast, Craven himself was part of the appeal. Jada Pinkett explains his hip factor by pointing out that most of the *Scream 2* cast were teens when *Nightmare on Elm Street* was released. "That makes Wes, like, a total hero."

The sequel picks up the action some time after the original killers were caught, and some of the survivors are now enrolled in the fictional Windsor College. Since the murders occurred, the sensational story has become national news, thanks to the true-crime book written by local television reporter Gale Weathers, again played by Courteney Cox. And in the American way, the book has been turned into a hit movie called *Stab*. When the youthful citizens of Woodboro go to see the movie, they take a *Rocky Horror* approach to moviegoing and dress up in the killers' masks. While the film recreates Drew Barrymore's untimely, messy demise in

Scream, a new murderer strikes and the nightmare for Sidney begins all over again.

Although most of the cast members, particularly the big names doing cameo appearances, were able to indulge in snappy one-liners and tongue-in-cheek dialogue, Neve's character played it straight. "That's why Sidney is so important in the film," Campbell explains. "You can have people around her being funny or being terrified, but the audience needs to believe *her* and see things from *her* eyes, so she has to remain real."

Co-star Courteney Cox had nothing but praise for the deceptively difficult acting job Campbell pulled off. "She had an extremely hard part in this movie, to be on the verge of fright and tears throughout and to keep it so interesting and real at the same time. She could do it," Cox says, "because she's grounded. She's a centered human being."

Never one to repeat herself too often, Campbell made it clear to Craven that she didn't want Sidney to be a victim. Neve tells Sherry Weiner of *UniverCity*, "Someone who's been through what she has either becomes suicidal or stronger and more determined, and that's how I decided to play her. She's been through an incredible amount of trauma in her life and needed to get away from her home town, develop new relationships, get involved in drama . . . help herself emotionally so she could forget — that's where I started with the character."

Instinctively, Neve understood that with "a scary film, you're dealing with extreme circumstances. So if they're not played in a realistic way and with some heart, it'll end up just a B movie. Sidney just had to persevere, no matter what, and become a stronger woman, not a victim, and really fight back, yet constantly question why her life is this way."

The location used for Windsor College was Atlanta's Agnes Scott College, where the production filmed for six weeks — in the middle of summer. Campbell told *Atlanta Journal and Constitution* reporter Steve Murray that when she wasn't working she and the others played pool and shopped, but added, "the heat there *is* a little harsh."

To cool off, the gaggle of actors took in the sights of Atlanta. "We seemed to make the decision early in the shoot to go to each bar in Atlanta — twice," Campbell says. About fifteen regulars "went out together as a group, a clique. It was so much fun."

Co-star O'Connell said the best part for him was going out with Campbell, Gellar, and Pinkett because "they could get in anywhere." The high profiles of the young actresses proved a point understood by a growing number of film executives. Mark Gill, marketing president at Miramax, explains. "Women are now driving the marketplace. You ignore this audience at your own peril." He points out that *Scream*'s primary audience was female and that they responded because the movie was actually a thriller, not a horror film. "It's got a good sense of humor; it's got Drew Barrymore and a lot of cute young boys. That does the job." Miramax was expecting *Scream 2*'s young female following to be just as large.

Being chosen as location for the film was a big coup for Atlanta, which already has a healthy film industry. "It's been a real spirit booster," said Agnes Scott College's dean of students, Gus Hudson to the *Atlanta Journal and Constitution*'s Jill Vejnoska. "No other film has sort of been in tune with the current generation of college students as much as this one, and we're very pleased with how Wes Craven treated our students and our campus."

After production wrapped at the Atlanta location, the cast and crew headed back to film the remaining scenes in Los Angeles. But because the filming overlapped with the start of *Party of Five*'s production, Neve found herself in the unenviable position of having to work double duty. The worst of it, Campbell recalls, was that "we were doing nights, so I would work until 5:30 AM, and only had an hour to rinse the blood off me before going to *Party of Five* and working all day. I almost lost it!"

In order to keep going, Neve told the *L.A. Times*' David Kronke, "you're actually better off not even questioning the length of time you have to not have a break. You have to learn to lie down when you have time to lie down, and how to save your energy and spend it when you have to."

Craven credited Neve's background for helping her push through her exhausting schedule. "I think because she's done theater, she just knows the concept of 'the show must go on' and the person is less important than the whole," the director suggested to Bernard Weintraub of the *New York Times*.

But more than just her work ethic was her ability to maintain personal balance. "There's just no bullshit about Neve," Craven colorfully told *Entertainment Weekly*. "She's the exact opposite of the kind of actress who has to run to her trailer every five minutes because her makeup's not right. She's got a real sense of what's important in life and has everything in perspective; like, for example, on the set she'd want to watch the sun set every night."

Neve's television series co-stars could only watch in amazement. "I don't think you can do everything she's doing and not be tired and frustrated sometimes," observed Scott Wolf. "But she's still Neve like I know her. She's still always laughing and smiling."

But those moments of levity belied the bone-deep weariness Campbell was experiencing. And it was not lost on her that she had those grueling years of dance training to thank for keeping her afloat. "I absolutely believe the reason I'm able to stay stable in this business, both psychologically and physically, is because of the discipline I learned there," she states. "It wasn't just the discipline, it was understanding the need to take care of yourself and realizing that if you want to be successful you must be prepared to do the work."

Perhaps one of the biggest ironies of Campbell starring in such a popular horror film is that she herself doesn't particularly care for the genre. "Not since I was a kid, just because I didn't believe in terrorizing myself and having nightmares all night. I saw *The Changeling* when I was a teenager and it's the scariest movie I ever saw in my life. I couldn't sleep a wink that night; I couldn't lie down, I couldn't budge. I had nightmares for a good year because of that movie. That movie still haunts me, maybe because I believe in ghosts and spirits," she admits. In fact, Campbell believes her own house is haunted, but by a good spirit. "A woman was murdered there five years ago. Once in a while the lights go really funky — and this is a brand-new house. Two people who were in my house saw her at the same time. But I believe it's good energy, so I don't feel weird in the house at all."

In Neve's world, the truly frightening things are more internal. "I used to have this really odd dream, when I was a kid, of jumping rope: Every time I tried to jump over the rope, I wasn't able to," she tells interviewer Jane Wollman Rusoff. "That was a recurring nightmare I had for a very, very long time. Maybe it was a fear of success, or a fear of not feeling I was capable."

Neve's subconscious worries about succeeding were shared by Kevin Williamson, who admitted he thought about whether everything was downhill from here. "I hope I'm not at the top of my game," he says. "I'm a work in progress." Although he became famous as a horror-movie reconstructionist, Williamson tells *Time*'s Michael Krantz, he has many other mountains he wishes to scale. "I want to do for action movies what *Scream* did for horror movies," he says. "I want to attack that genre; I want to kick its butt. And I want to do the same thing for romantic comedy. Scary, isn't it?"

In December 1997, *Scream 2* had the biggest December box-office weekend ever, crushing its cinematic competition with $39.2 million in ticket sales. Critics approved.

Needless to say, Miramax felt it had reason to crow, crediting the film's success with its multilayered appeal. "It's not just scary, it's not just fun, it's not just clever, it's not just a whodunit," said Miramax co-chair Bob Weinstein. "It's all that and it's something more. Like *The Crying Game* or *Pulp Fiction*, the Scream saga's a whole new approach to movies. It kills off all the old formulas."

While everyone was happy they had pulled off the improbable, Campbell mostly felt weary and unable to enjoy all the success she had earned. "I'm quite aware of the fact that I'm tired right now," she said. "But that's my choice, and I don't blame anyone but myself." It wasn't just a case of working for work's sake, though, Neve explained. It was so once *Party of Five* soaked its last tissue, "I can do two or three movies a year and have months off, and have my life."

Although Neve tends to dismiss the workaholic label, it got to the point where her body gave her a clear signal it was time to slow down. She developed an alarming case of alopecia, which is when your hair starts to fall out, often leaving unsightly bald patches —

Neve at the premiere of *Scream 2*

RUSSELL EINHORN / LIAISON AGENCY

not a happy thing for an actress. "I was working far too much and I wasn't getting enough sleep, so I started getting a bald spot on the back of my head," she relates to Jancee Dunn of *Cosmopolitan*. "An acupuncturist had to insert, like, twenty needles into my scalp to make my hair grow back."

It was no great secret that if Neve kept up the same breakneck schedule, she wouldn't be able to work at all, so since her bout with alopecia, she's tried to take better care of herself by sleeping as much as she can when the opportunity arises and getting regular acupuncture treatments. She also knows how important it is for her to "just sit and read some books and take a hike and light a fire and read for a little while."

And Neve had to continually adjust to the reality that she simply wasn't anonymous anymore, which brought an emotional fatigue all its own. "The bad aspects obviously are loss of privacy and feeling as though people want to create a persona for you that isn't necessarily who you truly are. It's a very odd thing when all of a sudden, your neighbors are telling you that people are taking pictures of you through your kitchen window.

"But on the other hand, if you handle it in the right way, you can also express who you truly are. I don't want to be one of those actresses who says she has no responsibility to her fans or the press, because I put my face out there every week. I can't be angry about the press. I don't understand celebrities who sit there going, 'The press sucks.' They have no right. The truth is, coming into this business, if you're going to put yourself in front of millions of people and choose to entertain them, it's a given people are going to be interested in you."

However, she also admitted to *USA Today* that at times she feels "like telling these people, 'Don't do this, don't knock on my door.' If you sit down and have a conversation with me, you'll realize I'm not as dramatic as you'd like me to be."

But that wasn't necessarily the case, as Neve was about to enter some particularly dramatic times.

10 A Hollywood Divorce

Although it was no secret to anyone that Neve had been working almost nonstop since *Party of Five* was given the green light in 1994, what few people knew was that her home life wasn't quite the fairy tale she projected. As late as the spring of 1997, in a very lengthy interview with *Australian TV Week*, Neve seemed the picture of marital bliss. When asked to compare herself with *Party of Five*'s sometimes wayward Julia, Campbell answered, "Julia is slightly confused. I am married and it's just great. Things in my real life couldn't be better. I just moved into my first house with Jeff and we're very, very excited. It's in the Hollywood Hills and I'm going to build a dance studio in it."

She also credited Colt with being the primary stabilizing factor in her life, during an interview with Anne Raso of *Australian Star*. "Reading about Buddhism and other paths to stability gets me through stressful days. And my husband Jeff keeps me sane. He's a great balancer in my life."

But it didn't take much digging to see another side of Campbell's marriage. It has been said in Hollywood that in two-actor marriages when the wife's career takes off before the husband's, the unions often break apart. Very seldom do you see Ms. Big Movie Star with Mr. Struggling Waiter or Mr. Hunk-in-Waiting on her arm. Whether it's because many women want to feel their partners are on equal footing with them or that the husband's ego can't quite cope with living in his spouse's shadow, it was no surprise to anyone that Jeff Colt, a struggling actor ten years older than Neve, might be having a hard time dealing with Neve's skyrocketing career.

Even Neve's brother Christian admits in an interview with Christopher John Farley of *Time* that "years ago, it was hard" being on the outside, looking in at a loved one succeeding in your field. "Because I was really struggling, having a hard time even feeding myself, and then to watch her get all this fame and money, I was, like, 'What is going on? What's going on in my life?'" However, as Christian proudly asserts, "Now I'm finding my own place." He learned to enjoy his sister's accomplishments without dwelling on his own perceived professional shortcomings.

Jeff Colt, whose most notable credit was appearing as a host on the Canadian program *It's Alive!* on YTV, never got to that place. Even in his praise, there was a tinge of bitterness, such as when he told *People* magazine, "She's able to do everything, so she wants it all."

Campbell was not oblivious to this pressure point. "Obviously, there are difficulties," she admitted. Then she added hopefully, "The most important thing is to communicate, talk it out, and you'll be O.K."

Because she had become not only a television star but a movie star as well, there was the added stress of constantly being in the public eye, even though, as Neve acknowledged, most people "have been respectful of our relationship. There are always people who aren't too concerned about your privacy and they'll interrupt a conversation or a romantic dinner, but that comes with the territory. People seem to be supportive, which is a wonderful thing."

Even though that loss-of-privacy issue seemed to loom like a pending rainstorm, Campbell refused to point a finger of blame at it. "I understand completely why, because when you choose to be an actor in this business you have to realize that it's basically giving your life to the public. But it's still intrusive in a lot of ways. People see you in a restaurant and don't want to come up to your table, so they'll go into the bathroom, because they think that's more appropriate, and they'll stand outside your stall and say, 'Can I get an autograph when you're finished in there?'"

The breaking point in her relationship with Jeff occurred while Neve was filming *Scream 2*. Court papers would later reveal that after two and a half years of marriage, the couple separated in July 1997. Campbell's representatives made the official announcement on July 30, although Colt's attorney, Franklin Garfield, wouldn't file divorce papers until November 6 of the same year. Friends, while sad for Neve, weren't surprised, because they knew that Campbell had always maintained a pragmatic view of marriage, saying more than once, "You try as hard as you can, and you love each other as much as you can, and you hope to grow together. You hope divorce is not an option. But if you're miserable, you know, together, then why continue?"

While some Hollywood divorces are played out in the media, Campbell refused to make this painful period of her life public. She politely but firmly refused to discuss the split, such as during an *E! Online* interview when she said, "I would really rather not talk about my relationship and my marriage. Jeff and I had our life together, and I love him very much still. That's its own circumstance, and that is private."

If there was one consolation in the backbreaking schedule of finishing *Scream 2* and starting the fourth season of *Party of Five*, it was that Neve was so busy she literally had no time to mope. And once she wrapped the film and returned to the regular series-shooting schedule, she found the *Party of Five* set a sanctuary where she could find peace.

Now single, Campbell immersed herself in her environment, getting it just the way she wanted it. One particularly cathartic outlet was decorating the new house she had bought while still with Jeff. "All of a sudden, I'm obsessed about houses and furniture," she said at the time. "I walk around the *Party of Five* set thinking, 'That's a nice table.'" Campbell also found solace in dance. In addition to taking some classes, she built a dance studio in her house: "I like to work in there and turn some music on."

But being single didn't mean being a party animal. Now when Neve went home, she found an empty house — which she considered preferable to hitting the singles bars. "It's really kind of the last thing you want to do after fifteen hours of work," she says. "I don't get into small talk. I have so little time to talk at all that if I do want to have a conversation, I'd like it to be deep and I'd like to learn something from it. What I really like to do is sit down with a friend, have a glass of wine, and have a great conversation about relationships, life, love, growth, the future, family — anything but talk about the industry." That kind of outlook is what prompts Christian to call his sister "a very grounded soul."

Whatever drama Neve had in her life would always pale in comparison to her television life. Those fans wondering what obstacles would be thrown in the Salinger clan's path were not disappointed by an emotionally wringing fourth season. Ironically, Campbell's character, Julia, found herself in a difficult marriage after having impulsively gotten married at the end of the third season. Everyone was aware of this art-imitating-life quality to the story line. Producer Amy Lippman points out that the writers were not exploiting Neve's personal situation, because the story line had been developed long before anyone knew Campbell and Colt were breaking up. That said, Lippman did note that she thought Neve's performance in the fourth season "has been informed by her own experience. She's very private and hasn't spoken about it on the set. She has not explained what of her own experience she's drawing from, but obviously some of it really resonates."

Neve admitted, without revealing anything, that it was a surreal experience. "It's odd timing. It's unfortunate timing. But it's O.K. That's what acting is — you take from your experiences and you put them on the screen. And I definitely have a lot to use. There are different circumstances and a different character, but I am able to take pieces of what my experience is and put it in there."

Sometimes when she talks about Julia, you can almost see Campbell analyzing herself. "In the past, I think I related to Julia even more because I was younger. Now I'm definitely feeling like I'm outgrowing Julia in a lot of ways. Once in a while I'm like, 'What is she doing?'" Neve says of Julia's bad choices. "But I have to go, 'Oh, right. I'm twenty-three, she's seventeen. I know exactly what she's doing.' But, on the other hand, Julia is pretty grown-up for her age and has had to deal with lots of adult situations in her life. She's had to grow up pretty quickly. And I definitely have gone through similar circumstances. So I do feel close to Julia in that."

Plus, as Campbell says, "I've been living her more than I've been living myself for the last five years. But she's not a very nice person this year. She's gone into college and she's making mistakes, that's for sure. And I don't like the mistakes she's making at the moment. But that's the show.

"There was a moment last season when Julia's telling Charlie why she just got married. He's very concerned, and she says, 'Charlie, look at me. I'm all grown up.' And I remember when I was seventeen and I was living on my own and I really believed I knew all about the world and that I had it all together. And now that I look back on that time, I think I knew nothing."

Julia's TV husband, Griffin, was played by actor Jeremy London, who in some ways should have felt right at home joining *Party of Five*. The series, noted for its searing melodrama, actually had nothing on London's real life. Jeremy and his twin brother, Jason, were born in San Diego, California, but grew up in Texas. In 1977, when the boys were just five years old, their parents, Debbie and Frank, who had married very young, divorced, and their mom supported them by working as a waitress. Emotional stability, however, proved much more difficult to provide. For a while after the divorce, Debbie and the boys lived on her father's ranch near Canadian, Texas. But her desire to try and find a better life for herself and her children prompted Debbie to keep on the move.

"Before the eighth grade, I probably went to seven or eight different schools," Jeremy recalls. "Often we would go to a school for just half or even a third of a school season and then move. You had to stay detached a little bit, because you knew that you probably were going to have to leave the friends you were making, the people you were getting close to. It was sad, to make friends with all these incredible people and then we'd be gone."

Neve with her former husband, Jeff Colt

© KATZ / LIAISON AGENCY

Perhaps because they were constantly uprooted, Jeremy says he and his brother grew up "begging for attention," which took the form of performing. "My first part was in this play we made up and did in our living room. I remember wrapping a towel around my head and jumping off the television set." Debbie, as it turns out, was less concerned with the fate of her furniture than with her children's psyche. "I always told them," she said to Mark Goodman of *People*, "we don't have the word *can't* in our vocabulary." But at times, *can't* seemed a way of life, until Debbie's faith was ultimately proved correct. One day in the restaurant where she was working, she met an actress who said she would put the twins in touch with her agent in Dallas. "Before that," says Jeremy, "we were doomed to redneckhood."

Or at the very least, a hardscrabble existence. At the time, Jeremy and Jason were living in DeSoto, Texas, a community just south of Dallas, with Debbie, her third husband, Roger Coffey, two of Roger's children, and their younger sister, Dedra, in a trailer. But almost immediately, the boys began going on auditions and, as it turned out, Jason struck Hollywood gold first in a movie called *The Man in the Moon*. Ironically, Jason hadn't been interested in trying out for the role, but Jeremy had insisted. "It was my audition," explains Jeremy, who said he genuinely didn't mind that Jason was hired because, as he told *People*, "I knew I'd be out there shortly."

In fact, Jeremy was hired to be his brother's stunt stand-in, and the experience was life-altering. "It was really the first time I'd ever been away from home," London told *TV Data*'s John Crook. "I got very close and emotionally attached to everyone on the movie, and when it was over, leaving was just heart-wrenching for me, one of the hardest things I've ever had to deal with in this business. Actors have to deal with that every day. You always have to be ready to move on."

But Jeremy would find that advice sometimes easier understood than done, especially when it came to parting from his brother. The occasion of their separation occurred in 1991, when Jeremy was hired for the role of Nathaniel Bedford on the NBC series *I'll Fly*

Away, which was filmed in Atlanta. Once again, though, it was a case of the brothers being interchangeable from a casting point of view. Jason had originally been hired for the role, but he turned it down because of a commitment to another show, filming in Los Angeles. It wasn't easy for Jeremy to be a continent apart from his brother, who he calls his womb mate. "It's the ultimate codependent relationship," noted Jason in *People*. So it's understandable that the first time they spent a significant amount of time apart was traumatic for them. "For him to be so far away definitely affected me," admitted Jeremy. "Every time I picked up the phone, he was about to call."

While many twins find great comfort in living under the same roof with their sibling, Jason and Jeremy discovered that once they grew up, they were much better suited as brothers and not roommates. Early in their career, when they were new to Los Angeles, the Londons moved in together, and the result, Jeremy tells Malissa Thompson of *Seventeen*, "was horrible. We've tried being roommates twice, but if we want to remain friends, we shouldn't be living together. I mean, when you're in a room with yourself, you'll go crazy, right? We had our wonderful times, but we're very different. I love him so much that I want to be able to get along with him. It's much better if we don't live together."

Jeremy London joined *Party of Five* as Griffin Holbrook in the second season, playing one of Julia's two love interests. Initially, Griffin was intended to be a temporary character — he was written out when he was sent off to military school after getting busted for stealing. "I was kind of disappointed about that," Jeremy admits. But due to the dramatic possibilities he presented and the fan mail he received, Griffin was brought back. "That made me feel really good," London tells Lisa Lombardi of *Twist* magazine. "It wasn't just girls who wrote in, which was kind of weird and surprising. A lot of guys identify with Griffin. They don't want to admit it but they like *Party of Five*, too."

Then, in a surprise story development devised by producers Keyser and Lippman, Julia and Griffin got married — to the shock of the fans as well as the fictional Salingers. But for the producers, it was a chance to explore just what it means to get married so young and to show dramatically why so many teen marriages end in divorce. For his part, Jeremy stated, "I don't believe people can be satisfied with their lives, taking on so much responsibility so early." He also noted, "I think teens get married so they can have sex all the time. But the whole sex thing will wear off quick."

London felt the marriage story line had good points and bad points. On one hand, he says, it was good that "Griffin got to grow up and become a man." But the downside was that in order to get the screen time, Griffin had to be married. "I don't think anybody should get married before they're thirty," he says, possibly thinking of his own parents. "You're too young to really know yourself." But, Jeremy notes, "Griffin's a bit of a ditz. I've never given him credit for having brains in his head."

Ironically, Jeremy himself had come very close to getting married young. When he was just twenty-two, London was engaged to actress Brittney Powell, but shortly before their wedding date, Powell called everything off. "It's depressing. I thought I was going to be with her for the rest of my life. She dumped me out of the blue," he says. "She didn't even give me my ring back. She just panicked and started treating me really bad, and it was obvious that she didn't want to be with me. It made me feel really bad about myself. She wound up really, really destroying me as far as the whole 'I love you' thing goes."

But as most people learn at some point in their lives, one door closing can often mean another door opening. Not long after breaking up with his fiancée, London was introduced to a competitive diver from Germany who helped mend his broken heart. "She's just good," he says. "Everything she does is right." That said, don't expect Jeremy to rush down the aisle right away. "People get carried away too easily," he comments. "I've been guilty of that. But my heart is just really guarded now. I could get married now, I'd be great at it, and I could have kids now. But I know for a fact that I'm not ready."

And for that, he says, he actually thanks Powell, because he says he realized after their relationship ended that he wasn't "ready to commit my life and soul to anyone yet. I used to be a hopeless romantic — I fell in love with everyone I went out with. Now I'm a little more jaded. I'm still in the process of learning who I want to spend the rest of my life with." That woman, says London, will be someone "who tells it like it is, no kissing up to me because I'm on TV."

Like Neve, London has aspirations behind the camera, although he's more shy about them than Campbell has been. He says he doesn't want to present anything for public consumption until he's absolutely, positively happy with it, because he'd "hate for people to degrade something I put my heart into." One such project is a script he's working on tentatively called *Bored*. "It's an intense movie about how awful drugs can be and where you can wind up if you're not careful," he explains. London got the idea after seeing friends lose themselves to drugs. "It's so sad," he says. "It drags you in, it drags you down. My point in the film is that you can make a decision about it. That's why I don't want to go out anymore. I don't want to see the people that I used to know who had their heads on good all screwed up on heroin. You see them now and they look like homeless people. I like myself enough that I don't feel the need to alter my existence."

Although *Party of Five* has been a positive experience for London, he does feel there were some missed dramatic opportunities that resonated with him personally, particularly when Griffin's sister was killed — an emotional devastation Jeremy had firsthand experience with. In 1991, his sixteen-year-old sister, Dedra — who was already married and the mother of a four-month-old baby — was killed in a car accident. Then, five years later, in an almost unbelievably cruel twist of fate, London's stepbrother was also killed in a crash. "That's one of the things in Griffin's past that is painful and powerful and poignant, just waiting to be used, but they don't seem to know what to do with it," London noted.

More than anything, his past has taught Jeremy that "you have to realize that your life is so important, and you need to love your brothers and sisters and your family," he tells *Twist*'s Lisa Lombardi.

"There is so much sibling rivalry in families, and people just take for granted every day that you'll all be there tomorrow."

As for where Jeremy sees himself tomorrow professionally, he comments, "If I am still doing what I'm doing and I still have respect in this town, haven't done anything completely and utterly stupid, then I'll be happy with myself."

For Neve, happiness would have been a less jam-packed daily dance card. However, the end was still not in sight for *Party of Five*.

11 Neve Wanderlust

With another long season looming ahead, and having just come off back-to-back movies, Neve seemed almost to wish the 1997–1998 season would be *Party of Five*'s last. "I love the show," she said at the time, "and it has done a lot for me, but I'm ready to move on. So, if it did get canceled, I wouldn't have a problem with it." Although he didn't get the same media coverage Campbell did, Matthew Fox voiced similar sentiments, saying that once his *Party of Five* contract was fulfilled, "I don't think I would do television again. The hours are unbelievable." Plus, for Fox, the steadiness of it went against his journeyman actor's soul. "Doing a television series, you know what you're going to be doing from week to week. I sort of like not knowing what's going to happen next. It's going to be cool to have that type of freedom again."

Nobody, though, seemed to pay much mind to Fox. It was Neve's comments that got the headlines and brought the most questions. Her co-stars seemed tolerant and understanding of the fact that she might allow their livelihoods to end so she could get on with her life. When asked at the Nickelodeon Kids Awards about Campbell's seeming desire to have the show canceled, Scott Wolf just laughed, saying, "That's Neve. She's always saying things like that."

Such as "Why do I stay on TV? A six-year contract. We're in our fourth year. I have two years left. I can't get out of it." Then, realizing how that must sound, Campbell catches herself. "And you know what? *Party of Five* has done a lot for my career. It's still a great job."

However, in the same breath she says that after the final two years, which would end in the spring of 2000, "That's it! Afterwards I only want to do features. Television is so grueling. Right now, although I'm tired, I realize I don't want to just do Julia. I want a career after the TV show is over. I want to be inspired. I need to challenge myself and I need audiences to be seeing me, so, if it means me doing two or three jobs at the same time, that's what I have to do."

In other words, Campbell didn't view her lifestyle as workaholic, merely as an investment in her future, a way of staying versatile in the public eye until she could put Julia in her past. In the meantime, the show went on. As the fourth season began, the Salingers were still feeling the repercussions from last season's dramatic high points, which included Scott Wolf's character, Bailey, being forced to admit he was an alcoholic — and having to deal with the knowledge his father had been one as well.

"It started with a young kid who needed to find himself somehow, and the thing that I love about him is he is a positive force," Wolf says. "He is a good, kind soul who, when given the option of trying to find an identity for himself, he chose to be the person who would take care of everyone. He chose to be the person who would hold everything together. And what is happening now is the pressures and the neglect of himself for the past couple of years are catching up to him."

In true *Party of Five* fashion, this isn't a problem that's solved by the end of an episode. "It's on television, so big, exciting things have to happen, and the question is, are you watching that to get some vicarious thrill, or do you watch it and say, 'Well, I understand that, that's what I've been through'?" asks co-creator and executive producer Christopher Keyser. "Bailey's issue with drinking started with episode one and took us seventeen episodes before somebody mentions it. The best thing we can do is lay these things in and make them feel like they're organic in a sense, that they come out of the characters and feel right at the time when they happen."

Then there was the matter of Julia's marriage. But remember, this is still just television and the thing that possibly shocked viewers most about the season premiere was seeing Julia get off the plane, after returning from a two-month sojourn in Europe, *with short hair.* Apparently, the mail came in fast and furious — *What had Neve done with her hair?* Um, it's called a haircut, folks. Coiffure aside, Julia comes back to deal with her relentlessly insecure husband, Griffin, while Charlie has to deal with his own issues when the family baby, Owen, develops a fancy for women's clothing.

Interestingly, Neve wasn't the only one feeling tinges of wanderlust. Behind the scenes, producers Keyser and Lippman had also discussed a weaning-away process from the series. "It's very hard to create your first show and watch it struggle and finally catch on, and then just walk away," admits Keyser.

Not that *Party of Five* was burning up the Neilsens. At the end of the third season, the drama ranked 82 among 125 series in households, but it also held second place behind ABC among the all-important eighteen-to-forty-nine-year-old demographic that is the golden cow of advertisers. That group of people, the industry believes, buys more products than any other, so a show high in that demographic commands more money for ads, making it more profitable for the network.

"You get used to feeling nervous about the ratings," says Keyser, who also possesses a law degree. "You learn to live with whether people watch or don't watch. You figure out how to get through, week by week. We don't plan our series around getting ratings. But we are beginning to feel more confident."

Certainly, though, life was easier going into their fourth season than it had been in years past. For example, News Corp. CEO Rupert Murdoch, in an effort to "help" *Party of Five*, called entertainment president John Matoian. Murdoch suggested that, since fire stories seemed to boost newspaper circulations, why not have the Salingers' house burn to the ground? Not only did Lippman and Keyser politely reject the idea, they sent Matoian a fire extinguisher as an exclamation point.

"Chris and Amy were always so unflinching about sticking with the vision," Matoian would recall later. "It was frustrating at times, but you'd think, 'Wow, these guys have an idea and are willing to go down with the ship if necessary.' And then you'd want to say, 'Well, maybe this ship is worth saving.'"

But it wasn't just the creators who showed great loyalty to *Party of Five*. "I don't think you can care too much," Scott Wolf told a somewhat cynical Dan Snierson of *Entertainment Weekly*. "I remember calling Amy Lippman once and leaving a message that said, 'Hey, it's me, Bailey. Gimme a call.' And her husband said, 'Does he actually like people to call him Bailey?' I guess I take what I'm doing very seriously."

Lippman, for one, appreciates the sentiment. "I'm sort of amazed at the extent to which everyone involved in the production still continues to care with that degree of intensity," she says. "So when you have that kind of enthusiasm, it makes it harder to walk away," especially because *Party of Five* was still so fertile dramatically. "There are still stories that we completely covet. One of the great things about creating your own show and staying on as executive producer is that you do get to pick the stories that you want to tell."

One of those stories involved Charlie's response to Julia's impromptu marriage, which for many episodes he emotionally refused to accept. During the November sweeps period, Keyser and Lippman developed a script that brought the family back together. "Charlie's saying, we never celebrated, so let's do something, you can resay your vows, whatever — it's just a way of saying publicly, 'We're a family and we're doing the wedding that we might have done if you had planned it and we all had said we're on board to begin with.'"

It's clear that Lippman and Keyser's passion is the engine that drives the series' continued quality. When considering how a season might begin, they ponder, "Where can we start them, and what path can we set them on that really shakes up the family dynamic?"

Julia's marriage was a case in point, "because we've never seen it before," says Keyser. "What happens when two eighteen-year-olds, who don't know who they are yet, decide to get married to each other? We'll take time and talk about what the experience of being married is when you're not even twenty. And there are a lot of people in this country who do that."

Julia continues to try and make her marriage work, and the family is rocked when Charlie develops cancer, which is diagnosed after he collapses while playing racquetball. Fortunately, it's a curable cancer, Hodgkin's disease, but terrifying nonetheless for siblings who have already lost their parents.

Naturally, though, not even the threat of cancer can bring the sibs together. Charlie's decision to tell each of his brothers and sisters about his illness separately leaves a trail of hurt feelings and misunderstanding. Claudia goes ballistic when she realizes Charlie wasn't totally honest with her about the seriousness of the illness, Julia explodes in anger when she hears the news secondhand, and Bailey just tries to stay sober. "It's going to be a long, long season for me," Fox said at the time. "It's incredibly difficult to put yourself in that emotional state. It's draining."

Some critics took issue with the fact that Charlie was given one of the most treatable forms of cancer, thereby minimizing his dramatic jeopardy. Fox pointed out that although Hodgkin's was "one of the most curable forms of cancer, one in four people who have it don't make it." (Coincidentally, former NBC entertainment president Brandon Tartikoff died of the disease in August 1997.) Part of the challenge for Fox was getting the look right, so he went on a diet to "get sort of gaunt-looking," putting himself in the emotional frame of mind to "go through what Charlie is going through."

Off-camera, Neve was going through more transitions of her own. In December 1997, gossip columns began running items that linked Campbell romantically to *Scream* co-star Matthew Lillard. "Campbell, who filed for divorce from actor Jeff Colt in November, has tried to keep her relationship with Lillard under wraps, but I feel safe in reporting that the actors are now very much a party of two," wrote one columnist. Not surprisingly, Campbell refused to comment one way or another about her love life, perhaps because her divorce from Colt was not final.

On the career front, meanwhile, Neve was expanding into new

areas. Earlier, ABC had signed Campbell to a development deal to star in a telefilm. But the network had let Neve break her commitment in order to shoot *Scream* — and in exchange she would executive-produce, cast, and star in a future project. Neve was pleased: "I want to have more control and I want to have more creative impact. Then you've got the whole thing."

The first idea Campbell thought of, a movie about Tourette's syndrome, was politely passed on by ABC, so she was still working to develop a project they could all agree on. Plus, she had filled her movie dance card for the coming hiatus and would once again go straight from *Party of Five* to a film set with no R&R time in between.

On May 8, 1998, the divorce between Neve Campbell and Jeff Colt became final. But in an unusual term of the dissolution, neither could publicly discuss their marriage, even in a "fictionalized" format. In other words, Neve made sure that in exchange for what was likely a hefty financial settlement from her — in California, all the money earned by spouses is added up and split down the middle, minus expenses — Colt could never write or sanction a tell-all tale of their relationship. According to the court documents, neither Campbell nor Colt could "publicly criticize, demean, malign or otherwise publicly comment disparagingly or negatively about the other party." Also neither was allowed to "publish or cause to be published any story, article, column, comment, book (fictionalized or nonfiction) describing the other party or the marriage of the parties." Beyond all that, the agreement stipulates that "each party should use all reasonable efforts to discourage family members, friends and other acquaintances" from publicly discussing — in other words *dissing* — either of the estranged spouses.

Despite the unfortunate outcome of her relationship with Colt, the experience hadn't turned Neve off of actors as potential mates. "It's an odd thing," she muses. "Actors have the same schedule, so they're more understanding. How many people who work nine to five would understand why I work fourteen- to sixteen-hour days and travel every other weekend or travel four to five months at a time? But another actor will understand that."

And while Neve may have been testing the dating waters with former co-star Lillard, it would be a while before she would become seriously involved with anyone. For the time being, her most faithful lover would continue to be her work.

By the late 1990s, enough time had passed in America that our culturally imbued desire for all things nostalgic turned its lonely eyes towards the disco era. The Fox network was developing a series about the post-flower-child era, *That 70s Show*, which would become a surprise hit for their network. At the same time, books about the notorious disco hotspot Studio 54 and its famous and infamous denizens were hitting the racks. So it wasn't surprising that down the pipeline came the film *54*, about club co-owner Steve Rubell's den of disco iniquity.

Shot mostly in Toronto, *54* gave Neve the chance to go back home and work with a cast that, at least on paper, seemed ideal. Starring as Rubell, who died in 1989 from AIDS-related complications, was fellow Canadian Mike Myers. Although his role was dramatic, Myers, who's inherently funny, kept the cats loose in between takes. The film also featured Salma Hayek, who said of Campbell, who played a soap-opera actress, "I gotta say, for being a Canadian, she's a hell of a salsa dancer." Hayek, portraying a coat-checker/would-be disco queen, bonded with Neve and the two hung out together during the month-long shoot. The young male lead was Ryan Phillippe, who had earlier scored big in the Kevin Williamson-penned movie *I Know What You Did Last Summer*.

Considering the cast and the timely nature of the movie's story matter, *54* seemed like a really good idea when production began. The basic premise went like this: Shane, a young kid from New Jersey, is seduced by the all-the-sex-and-drugs-you-can-consume hedonism of Studio 54. Director and screenwriter Mark Christopher had done five years of research to construct a detailed and accurate script that didn't shy aware from the ugly excesses and indulgences of the real Studio 54. Unfortunately, his script was a little *too* real for the brain trust at Miramax. And after the movie tested badly, it was ordered reshot, was reedited and, in the end, bore little resemblance to what Christopher had originally written.

The lightning rod for much heated discussion was the central story of the film. In Christopher's optioned script, the crux of the plot was a love triangle between Ryan Phillippe's Shane — who maneuvered his bare-chested self into a job as a club bartender — and the married couple Greg and Anita — Breckin Meyer and Salma Hayek. There were serious homoerotic overtones as not only did Shane sleep with Anita, he also shared a kiss with Greg. And, of course, there were plenty of drugs to hasten Shane's downfall, which would end with him being expelled from the club alongside Greg and Anita, whose marriage he had destroyed.

Miramax purchased the *54* script in 1997 and, after overseeing minimal rewrites, sent the director and his cast to Toronto for the two-month fall shoot. There, Christopher filmed a story about an out-of-control love triangle set against the backdrop of an out-of-control nightclub. After the opening scenes, in which Shane is plucked off the street and given a bartending job at the club, Christopher's original script has him spiral downward, not only indulging in drugs but also undermining Greg and Anita's marriage. All the characters engage in tawdry behavior as they claw their way to the top of the heap of creeps, culminating in Shane's expulsion from the club. But he, Greg, and Anita leave together, apparently having found happiness with each other.

The problem with the film was its internal schizophrenic nature. While its cast was top-heavy with teen-friendly faces, such as Phillippe, Campbell, Myers, and Hayek, the subject matter was intense and dark. Not surprisingly, the film tested poorly with its targeted teen audience. According to studio insiders, audiences found nothing at all redeeming about Shane in particular and were seriously turned off by the implied meaning of the ending.

But when word leaked out that Miramax had insisted the kissing scene between Shane and Greg be cut, it seemed proof that the studio's real objection lay in the film's homoerotic elements. However, even a cursory look at the Miramax history, which includes

The Crying Game, makes that argument spurious. A weary Christopher offered this analysis to Rebecca Ascher-Walsh of *Entertainment Weekly*: "This was a very ambitious story line from the start. Our goal was to keep the audience sympathetic to the characters, and any material that was removed from the film was removed because it was too challenging for some members of the audience. However, I'm excited because some of the most groundbreaking material really played and still remains."

Later, Christopher would alternate between feelings of betrayal at the hands of Miramax and a resignation at learning the lessons of moviemaking the hard way. "The process is . . . whatever. Can we keep this general? We were both trying to make the best movie possible, and I think we've done that."

In the end, when *54* was released, the love triangle between Shane, Greg, and Anita was gone. Taking up more screen time suddenly were Campbell and Meyer, whose roles were originally quite small. To fill the gaps, a voice-over narrative by Shane was dubbed in and his relationship with Neve's soap-opera actress was heightened. The result was a pieced-together smorgasbord of celluloid looking for a story. Some of the actors, such as Mike Myers and Campbell, shrugged off their losses and moved on to the next project. Others, like Ryan Phillippe, who had much more riding on the film, couldn't help but express disappointment.

"It's pretty frustrating to go into something with the best intentions and interests, and have to let it go at a certain point because I'm not the one investing the money," he said. Hayek colorfully chalked it up to one more Hollywood learning experience: "A lot of my scenes got cut, but shit happens."

Campbell's celluloid life, on the other hand, smelled like roses.

12 A Learning Experience

Neve

Although Neve seemed genetically incapable of turning down work, some jobs were clearly more fun than others. One calm and stress-free experience for Campbell was "appearing" in the Disney made-for-video release *Lion King II: Simba's Pride*, playing the grown-up Kiara, Simba's daughter.

In the film, which is populated by animated lions, Simba has comfortably settled into his role as leader of the pride but is less surefooted as a father. Having once been a rebellious cub himself, Simba has grown into an overly protective parent, but not without reason. At the outskirts of Simba's realm lies the Outlands, a barren area ruled by Zira, who is determined to avenge the death of her former mate, Scar, Simba's evil uncle who died at his nephew's paws. To achieve her revenge, Zira has carefully trained her son, Kovu, to kill Simba so Zira can take over Pride Rock. Nala and Simba's daughter, Kiara, voiced by Campbell, meet and a blossoming romance ensues. But their mutual efforts to bring the two feuding prides together only result in getting them both banished. In the end, however, evil is once again conquered and Kiara and Kovu take their place as the new generation of pride royalty.

While Neve may enjoy showing *Simba's Pride* to her children in later life, the experience surrounding *Hairshirt* brought much more immediate fulfillment. *Hairshirt* was a small-budget film that was literally a family affair. Along with her brother Christian and two friends, Dean Paras and Katie Wright, Neve produced and appeared in the ultra-independent film, written and directed by

Paras. Neve plays a famous film and TV star who'll stop at nothing to destroy her friend's love life.

"You never want to be that way as a human being," she said, "but it's certainly fun to play on camera — and get away with it." Even so, the insecure part of Neve admitted, "I had a bit of apprehension that people would make the assumption that that's actually me, because she is a television and film star. But I played the role so extreme and it is such a comedic role that I'm hoping people don't make that assumption. But she's hilarious," Neve said of her nasty character, "and so catty. I'm so glad that I'm not that person in the film. But it's fun to play up your dark side. She's the kind of girl you just want to slap and wake up. I just really love the movie. It makes me laugh no matter how many times I see it, because I love the characters so much."

It was particularly special for Neve to premiere the film at the Toronto International Film Festival. "I love this city," she said at the time. "I'm very proud to be a Torontonian and to be able to premiere the film here in front of our friends and family, and everyone's so enthusiastic, it's fantastic."

For Neve, *Hairshirt* was an opportunity to learn more about the business of moviemaking, an interest she'd been cultivating. "Christian and I had been wanting to produce for a while," said Neve. "We'd gone to a Martin Scorsese tribute in L.A. a couple of years ago and realized that the same people had worked basically in all of his movies — he kept his movie family very, very tight." The idea of a familial film troupe was appealing to both Campbells. "We have this pool of talented friends who we really believe in, and I'm in a position where I can create that, so why not? Why not bring all these people together and create something? And two days after that conversation, Dean and Katie came to us and said we have this film. It was perfect timing, really symbiotic.

"It was so nice to have more creative control on a project as opposed to just being a puppet and showing up and doing the lines. It was more about calling the shots." It was also about work. "It was definitely a lot more work than we had imagined," Neve admits about the production. "And it offered a huge amount of challenges. I learned a lot and really have an appreciation for producers now, that's for sure. But on the other hand, it was an amazing experience. I think because we were all new at it, there was a great amount of enthusiasm. For me it was like going to film school for four years. We had a lot of creative control and we were able to help each other out. We were all very humbled by the experience and realized that we were all learning. It was a team effort."

It might have been a team effort, but it was Neve's stellar standing in the movie business that paved the way for bigger projects in the future. "I'm lucky enough to be in a place where I have the kind of name where studios are saying, 'We'd like to make a film with you.' So why not go and find a book and a writer, and put something together and make it happen, as opposed to waiting for a studio to come along with a great script?" But before jumping in too deep, Campbell says she "wanted to start very simply and from the bottom and actually learn about everything. I don't think many actors want to become producers, because we just see producers running around yelling, and who wants that? If you can see it as putting together a really complicated jigsaw puzzle, once it's together, you've accomplished something."

Hairshirt's festival premiere in Toronto in September 1998 was intended to attract a distributor for the movie. Again, with Neve's name attached, there was no shortage of buyers present, leaving Christian in the celluloid clouds. "I couldn't be excited, I couldn't be upset," Christian says of his emotional state that night. "I didn't know what to feel. I was numb."

While *Hairshirt* was potentially a big step in Christian's life, for Neve it was more like fine-tuning. Adding a producer's credit to her résumé was just further evidence that she was really and truly a grown-up now. "I do not want to play teenagers much longer," she told *Toronto Sun* reporter Bruce Kirkland. "Julia will be twenty when I'm twenty-six. I want to play my age and I've started doing that in my other roles. No matter how good you are as an actor, you grow up. Your face grows up."

And your priorities change. Earlier in her career, Neve might have felt compelled to attend a film's wrap party, but when *Hairshirt* threw its end-of-filming soiree, she begged off. "I really needed to just sit and read books, take a hike and light a fire," she explained.

As *Hairshirt* was being promoted and making the exhibitor rounds, Neve was back at work on the fifth season of *Party of Five*. What few outside of Hollywood knew was how close the series had come to winding up on another network. In the middle of the previous season, Fox had unexpectedly balked at the licensing fee *Party of Five*'s producers were asking — $2 million per episode, double the fee paid for the fourth season. If Fox didn't come to some kind of agreement with the series' producer, Columbia TriStar TV, by February 18, 1999, the studio would have been free to shop the series to the other networks. And with television dramas a highly valued commodity, a bidding free-for-all would have ensued. For all of Fox's griping, relatively speaking, the $2 million licensing fee they paid to hang on to *Party of Five* was a bargain — especially when one considers that NBC had to pony up a staggering $13 million to keep *ER* from going elsewhere. And in the end, cooler heads prevailed and an agreement was reached that would keep *Party of Five* on Fox through the 1999–2000 season.

While this made fans happy, Neve was still feeling torn about the series. She realized that she had the series to thank for her film opportunities, but it was hard not to lament what might have been. Reportedly, Campbell had been forced to turn down the role that ultimately went to Liv Tyler in *Armageddon* because it conflicted with her *Party of Five* schedule. "It's very frustrating," Campbell admits, "but the reason I'm getting the offers is *Party of Five*, and I have to appreciate what I have. You have to know that there is a possibility that it will go a long time," she says of signing on to a series. "You take that chance. If I'm gonna be stuck in a six-year contract, this is the one I'd want to be on."

Neve had also shown interest in *Rounders*, a Miramax film to be directed by John Dahl. But Miramax, which also owned the *Scream* films, told her that if they cast her in *Rounders* she would have to agree to star in *Scream 3* for a salary of $3 million. Low by action-hero standards but high for Miramax films. However, not enjoying the sensation of being railroaded, Campbell turned down the conditional offer. Adding words to her show of flexed muscle, she said, "Apart from not wanting to be a *Scream* queen, as ironic as that is, I also want to expand my career. I want to feel challenged and to be playing all kinds of characters. If it comes down to it on my hiatus, and I have three months, and it's a choice between *Scream 3* and another film, I will do the other film."

Adding to Bob and Harvey Weinstein's consternation was that Wes Craven had already gone on record saying if Neve didn't return, neither would he. While the Miramax founders pondered how to save the third installment of their *Scream* trilogy, Campbell busied herself in the weekly demands of her television series, which stirred up further controversy at the end of its fifth season when Julia exchanged erotic embraces with another woman. However, anyone expecting *Wild Things* for the small screen was to be disappointed. In the episode, Julia and her friend Perry — a former Stanford student and visiting professor in her writing class played by Olivia d'Abo — find themselves locked in a tender but erotic kiss.

"Audiences have become more sophisticated, even in the last few years, and so television is becoming more realistic," says Marcia Schulman, senior VP of talent and casting for Twentieth Century Fox Television. "That's the beauty of these teenage ensemble shows; there's something for everybody, so you can add a gay character to the mix. It's a great trend. Actors are finally choosing roles based on how well they're written and how interesting they are to play, not on whether the character is gay or straight."

Media analyst Marc Berman acknowledges that "it is risky" to introduce gay story lines, but he also says networks such as "the WB and Fox made names for themselves by taking risks. While we're seeing more gay themes, overall the media response has been very positive. And even if there is a protest, that can mean increased ratings."

In the case of *Party of Five*, it turned out to be much d'Abo about nothing, except maybe a way to get a slightly larger audience sampling. "Maybe people who don't normally tune in to the show will watch because they'll think, 'Oh, this is something spicy,'" suggested d'Abo. "And they'll end up seeing something wonderful — a very sweet, honest, earnest relationship between these two women who have nothing but genuine respect for each other." The kiss, explained d'Abo, occurs after Julia "just plants one on Perry spontaneously after we have this hug, like how you'd kiss anyone on the lips out of joy. Then we both realize it feels kind of good, and we kiss again. Then we're in an awkward place like, 'What's gonna happen now?'"

The short answer — nothing. "There's no big lesbian affair," d'Abo told Shawna Malcom of *Entertainment Weekly*. "We do share one rather nice kiss, but, like, get over it already."

Even so, Neve enjoyed breaking the Julia mold just a bit. "With blondes, the assumption is that they're blonde bombshells and it's all about sexuality," she mused. "With brunettes, they're considered the quiet types, the more innocent types, the more intelligent types. I don't mind being intelligent, it's fine. But it doesn't necessarily mean I always have to be innocent."

In November 1998, *Party of Five* aired its one-hundredth episode. Considering how bleak the future had looked for the series in its first season, few were more amazed than the creators, Christopher Keyser and Amy Lippman. In fact, Keyser admits that he had originally thought he'd have been happy to get ten episodes on the air. "I was never so glad to be totally wrong," Keyser adds.

It's no secret that for many series, the one-hundred milestone can be the beginning of the end, a fact not lost on Keyser. "It becomes harder and harder not to repeat yourself and to come up with plots that are believable," the producer told Dennis Hunt of *USA Today*. "It helps that these characters are young," he adds. "They all go through growth stages that seem natural and inspire believable story lines."

And indeed, the fifth-season dramatics still seemed to be resonating with the faithful *Party of Five* viewers. With his cancer apparently behind him, Charlie was now expecting a baby with girlfriend Daphne. But after baby Diana is born, Daphne leaves, believing it is in the baby's best interest. Bailey has taken over running the family restaurant while both maintaining his sobriety and being supportive to Sarah, who suddenly finds her own family life turned upside down. Over the season, he and Sarah will examine and re-examine their relationship, before moving in together.

Claudia, languishing in boarding school out of state, becomes so homesick that she sets out to get herself expelled, but is ultimately brought back home by Julia's estranged husband, Griffin, who is resistant to signing the divorce papers. For a brief while, he and Julia seem to be on the verge of reuniting, which causes mixed emotions in Claudia, who admits to a friend she's fallen in love with Griffin. Not even toddler Owen escapes trauma in the fifth season, as he becomes the focus of a divisive custody battle between Bailey and Charlie.

Julia's love life is as star-crossed as ever. After her separation from Griffin, she breaks the cardinal rule of roommates when she begins to date her roomie's boyfriend, Ned. But Ned isn't the benign guy he seems at first, which Julia discovers when he hits her after she refuses to move out of her room and in with him. This particular story line disturbed not only viewers but also critics, who worried that perhaps the wrong message might be inferred.

During a commercial break, Campbell was featured in a public service announcement about relationship abuse, but some felt the character's actions spoke louder than Neve's words. One of the series' producers, John Romano, was quick to defuse any controversy. "It's meant to be disturbing," Romano said. "You don't want to tell people that the feelings inside the emotions don't exist."

Keyser and Lippman consulted experts to assist in developing the story line and, according to Romano, they "were all very clear that we couldn't do the short version" of working through an abusive relationship. Consistent with the show and Julia's character, she

Neve at the Family Film Awards in L.A., 1996

FITZROY BARRETT / GLOBE PHOTOS

would eventually accept the painful truth of the situation and make the break, in the process becoming a much stronger person. As for her feelings about the story line, Campbell opted for neutrality. "Well," she offered, "they have to find something else to do with the character."

For as much as the trials and tribulations of the Salingers kept their fans happy, it was *Party of Five*'s lack of top-ten success that may have actually helped maintain its longevity, according to ad buyer Paul Schulman, president of Schulman/Advanswers NY. "It was never huge in the ratings, but it has always scored high among the viewers that advertisers want to reach," Schulman says, specifically citing the female 12–34 and 18–49 demographic, "and that's what has kept the show on the air."

When the fifth season drew to a close, Charlie had been reunited with Kirsten, who had agreed — again — to marry him; Bailey and Sarah were coming to the painful realization that their lives were heading in different directions; Claudia was learning hard lessons of her own about the real keys to being popular; and Julia made herself and her family proud by winning a fellowship for the following year.

While it seemed as if the saga of the Salingers could go on forever, the reality was that *Party of Five* was about to enter what quite possibly would be its last season. Certainly, as far as Neve was concerned, it was *her* last season. "April 2000," she said pointedly, "and then I'll have a life."

13

Neve

One Last *Scream*

In May 1999, Neve Campbell finally ended the speculation and agreed to star in the third and, definitely for her, final installment of *Scream*, teaming up again with Courteney Cox, David Arquette, and director Wes Craven. Kevin Williamson, however, wound up not penning the final script because by June he had written only about thirty pages, having spread himself way too thin — he was in the middle of postproduction on *Mrs. Tingle* as well as working on his new ABC series, *Wasteland*.

"I had two weeks to write it, and I just wasn't capable of doing it," he admits. "Everyone was frustrated with me, and it was a big sore spot. I crashed and burned. I got so overloaded that I called Bob Weinstein in tears and said, 'I just can't do it. Can we push this movie to next year?' I gave all the reasons I felt it should be pushed — because of all the violent stuff going on in the world. But they had already locked in Courteney and Neve and it was impossible to push it."

Campbell in particular was worried because she didn't want the production delayed so it would once again overlap her *Party of Five* commitment. So Williamson turned over the franchise and his idea to Ehren Kruger, who wrote the *Scream 3* script, now said to be "loosely based" on an idea by Williamson.

Once again, out of necessity, the plot of *Scream 3* was another closely guarded secret. Producer Cathy Konrad spoke of the film in broad, vague terms. "Our kids have graduated," she said. "It's not a high school movie; they can't be in high school forever. They have to move on in their lives. So the story is taking a natural arc with what they've been through and how they've grown up. The first one was in Woodsboro. The second one was in college. And now they're in the world. So the story has to progress; otherwise, the audience would be disappointed."

However, fans expecting another holiday opening for *Scream 3* would be disappointed. Because of the production delays, the final installment of the trilogy wouldn't open until February 2000. "It was going to be excruciating," director Wes Craven said of trying to open for the Christmas movie rush. So Miramax executive Bob Weinstein stepped in, saying, "You've hit a home run! It's ridiculous to rush it."

Craven took to task Internet sites that featured the alleged plot, which has Neve's character, Sidney Prescott, going Hollywood, becoming an actress, and starring in yet another movie based on the murderous events in her life. "That story line has been erroneously reported and is not actually the plot at all," Craven complained during a *Fangoria* interview. What he would allow was, "There is a picture being made as part of our story, which is one of the sequels in the *Stab* series, the movie within the movie. Sidney does get involved in it, but not as an actress. *Scream 3* deals very much with the reality of one's life and the way the media tends to treat reality as a sensationalist object. But obviously we're not rushing to clarify people's misconceptions about it."

Joining the *Scream* alumni for the third installment were co-stars Lance Henriksen, Parker Posey, Scott Foley, Patrick Dempsey, and Jenny McCarthy. Now that Sidney is out of college, Craven describes her as "a completely independent young women who is trying to deal with the trauma of her past and put it to rest. There's a kind of completion of the circle in this film. We're going back to some of the original story and offering new revelations so all the elements of the three films will kind of fall into place."

Along with Campbell, also returning from the first two films were David Arquette and Courteney Cox as Deputy Dewey and reporter Gale Weathers. In the second film, Dewey and Gale rekindled the flirtation started in the original. "In this one, we don't have a tra-la-la romance between Dewey and Gale that we more or less had in the first two films," Craven says. "There is now more of a maturing relationship."

Just as Neve's *Party of Five* story line with Griffin seemed to reflect her real-life marital situation with Jeff Colt, the on-screen relationship between Dewey and Gale was a case of art imitating life. The two used the *Scream* films as an unorthodox backdrop for an unorthodox courtship that culminated in their June 1998 wedding, which took place just a few days before the principal photography began on *Scream 3*. Although Arquette says it was love at first sight, this, however, was no whirlwind, impulsive romance.

When Cox and Arquette met at a pre-*Scream* dinner at director Wes Craven's house, David could feel his heart flip. And as the filming progressed, it became obvious that Courteney was just as drawn to Arquette. While both had been involved in high-profile relationships previously — Cox enduring a very public breakup with ex-fiancé Michael Keaton, Arquette having been linked with Ellen Barkin — neither was then seeing anyone. But the road wasn't as clear as it seemed on the surface, a fact understood by Wes Craven, who gave Arquette some fatherly advice. David tells the *Dallas Morning News* that Craven said, "David, I know Courteney really loves you a lot and it's sort of up to you to make the decision of what you want to do. I just want you to know that you're a great guy and she's a great girl and I think you'd make a wonderful couple. It's going to take you getting your life together and working it all out and choosing the right path. But I think it would be a great thing for you guys to do."

Craven was alluding to Arquette's reputation as a heavy partier. Actually, it was more than mere reputation, as David freely admits to Louis B. Hobson of the *London Free Press*. "My addictions made it difficult for us to have a proper, lasting relationship," Arquette says bluntly. "I desperately wanted a serious relationship, but that's impossible when you're as messed up as I was."

So their budding romance came up short, but with no hard feelings, as it was understood Arquette was going to try and conquer his demons, which he believes had their genesis in his peripatetic childhood. As the children of actors, the Arquette kids often endured a hardscrabble life. "My parents always told us show business is a difficult world, and it wasn't an easy life. We grew up from month to month, day to day," David recalls. "We didn't grow up with anything we wanted or anything close to that. There were often long periods between my father's jobs. We'd often run out of food and get IOU's at Christmas. The reason we Arquettes can play trailer trash so well is that we learned it first-hand."

At the urging of his family, Arquette turned to acting, and as his credits grew, so did his flirtation with drugs. Although he told *USA Today*'s Stephen Schaefer, "I never got *too* deep in it," he was in deep enough that "I call those my free-fall years. People got really frightened for me. Family members tried to intervene, but I wouldn't let them. My poor mom didn't know what was going on and I didn't, either. I was so messed up. All I know is that I didn't want to deal with it."

When Cox and Arquette found themselves co-starring in *Scream 2*, the old feelings flared back up. "We immediately reconnected, but because I was at a big crossroads in my life, we never committed." However, tragedy brought them back together when, in 1997, David's mother, Mardi, died of breast cancer. "Losing her was the hardest thing I've ever had to cope with," says Arquette. "Without Courteney, I know I couldn't have coped. All through the whole thing, she was there as a friend. That's when I noticed what it would take to be with her and have that life. She didn't make it a condition of our friendship, but I knew if I wanted to stay with Courteney, I had to clean up my act."

After checking himself in for rehab and starting therapy, Arquette began to feel he was finally taking back control of his life. In September 1997, while he and Courteney were visiting her parents in

Florida, David proposed. The thing that seems to amaze Arquette the most is that Cox "didn't give up on me just because I'd given up on myself. I was actually shocked that when the smoke finally cleared, she was still there."

When asked if working together on *Scream 3* was different now that they were married, Cox jokes, "I mean it's great. Sure there's been days where we just thought, 'Maybe you shouldn't come today,' but it's just nice. It's nice to work together."

Contrary to some published reports, Craven says that his trio of core actors, Campbell, Arquette, and Cox, had always been willing to do the final film. The problem, he says, wasn't one of lack of interest or desire, but of scheduling. "We were dealing with a group of actors who are very busy. But there was willingness on the part of everyone to do the third one. Nobody believes us, but there is not going to be another *Scream* after this, and so there was the added incentive on everybody's part to finish what they started."

A more pressing potential problem the filmmakers had to struggle with, in this post-Columbine world, was whether it was socially responsible to even make *Scream 3*, which was originally due to open in December 1999. With the millennial year 2000 being a presidential election year in America, the politicos would likely use Hollywood as the whipping boy for all the country's violent tendencies — especially in the wake of a sensational 1998 killing in the Los Angeles area. A teenage boy, Mario Padilla, along with an accomplice, had killed Padilla's mother by stabbing her forty-five times. The teens told authorities they had got the idea from the two *Scream* films. The mother's killing was to be the first of many. With her dead, they could steal money, buy outfits like the *Scream* killer's and voice-altering equipment, then set about killing students in their high school.

Anti-Hollywood forces were anticipating the case to be an indictment of Hollywood as a whole, until Judge John J. Cheroske ruled that the defense would not be allowed to introduce *Scream* into evidence. In addition, Cheroske barred Court TV and CBS from broadcasting the proceedings. Although the judge declined to explain his decision, he did note, "This case is not to be referred to as the *Scream* case." (In 1999, both boys were convicted. Padilla was sentenced to life imprisonment without parole, and his accomplice, who was only fourteen at the time of the killing, received twenty-five years to life.)

Despite finding themselves in the eye of such a political and societal storm, the producers and Miramax maintained they would not be censored and would remain true to the first two films. "I have a conscience, but I don't think that in the spirit of entertainment, you can take it to the point where you're censoring yourself," Cathy Konrad tells television journalist Pat O'Brien. "Sometimes the way in which a story is told can really speak to the climate of what people are talking about. If we let the climate alter our artistic desires and whims, then we're in for a pretty ugly world."

She goes on to point out that "horror movies are part of cinema history. They've been around and defined for a long, long time. We're not breaking new ground. And there's an audience for them — people who love to be scared. If you talk to Wes, the psychology of the release in a theater, to be able to be afraid or scream, is just part of human nature. And it's fun."

Director Craven acknowledges that while there were some concerns, the filmmakers believed they weren't exploiting the national preoccupation with teenage violence. In addition to the film's change of environment away from academia, Craven also points out that, in his opinion, "the films talk about responsibility. [In *Scream 3*], we talk about personal responsibility as the only way to have a society run right. We feel we've always been responsible. The killers have all been losers, and Neve is a really decent human being. She doesn't smoke, drink, or do drugs. We've always gone with a central character that is straight up with courage."

For Neve, filming *Scream 3* was the end of a special chapter in her life. "Am I gonna miss it? Yeah, it's kind of like giving birth. *Scream* has been fantastic for me. I had a lot of fun doing the first two movies and they don't take themselves seriously. And I like that."

The experience was bittersweet for Craven. "On the one hand, we were just going about our business of making a good scary movie," the director says. "But I couldn't help but think about the fact that this would be the last time I would be dealing with Neve, Courteney, and David in this context. These characters and circumstances were never going to be played out again. It's a weird feeling. But there's also the good feeling of completing a classy series of films."

After *Scream 3* wrapped, there was rampant speculation that Craven would use the film as his horror-genre swan song and move into more mainstream fare, such as his post-*Scream* project *Music of the Heart* with Meryl Streep. Although he seems to be struggling with the issue himself, it's unlikely Craven would ever completely walk away from the genre he has helped mold.

"If I left horror for good, I would miss the fun and sense of adventure involved in making the films," he admits. "I would miss the challenge of keeping ahead of the sharp young audiences that horror seems to embrace. So I guess I won't be completely leaving the genre. I'll just keep updating the act."

14 Neve
"A Job That I Love"

Although Neve was far less taxed during the filming of *Scream 3*, in many ways her life was fuller than it had ever been. In May 1999, Campbell presided over the annual Tourette Syndrome Foundation of Canada's annual fundraiser. "I'm producing an educational tape for Tourette's syndrome because educating the public about it is very important to me," she said, explaining her commitment to the foundation's efforts.

She was also on hand to cheer on her brother Christian for his performance in the independent film hit *Trick*, in which he plays Gabriel, a gay man trying in vain to find some time alone with a one-night stand, who turns out to be much more like the man of his dreams. As it happened, Tori Spelling played Christian's ever-present best friend who keeps upsetting Gabriel's plan for a sexual tryst with go-go dancer Mark.

Trick received critical acclaim, and so did the cast, particularly Campbell and Spelling. For Tori, who's frequently been singled out for unflattering comments because of the perception that she has a career only because her father is ubiquitous television producer Aaron Spelling, it was sweet vindication. "I think I've been doing good acting on *90210* for ten years, but they dismiss that because it's my father's show," Spelling told Joey Guerra of the *Houston Chronicle*. "People's perception is really weird. No one wants to see you get ahead, but all of a sudden you do one thing that's completely different and has nothing to do with your dad, and they're like, 'Oh wow, now she's good.' I've had to deal with it for so long that I kind of just got hardened to it. At first it hurt, and it was hard to deal with. Then, I kind of got the attitude like, 'I'm going to just try really hard and do really great work, and then they won't be able to say it anymore.' Now, I'm over it. I don't care what people say."

For Christian Campbell, the success of *Trick* made him contemplate what it would be like to enjoy his sister's level of success. "I question whether I want Neve's kind of superstardom in my life, he told the T*oronto Sun*'s Bob Thompson. "Sometimes she's in tears on the phone to me because she's had her life taken away from her. I'm hoping to get to a place where I have balance in my life, where I'm doing things *and* enjoying them."

Neve says the desire to lighten things up a bit was at the root of her decision to star in 1999's *Three to Tango*, a comic farce also featuring Matthew Perry and Dylan McDermott. "I wanted it badly. I'd done my fair share of crying on *Party of Five* and screamed my way through *Scream* movies, when I read *Three to Tango*. My audience and my critics have said they'd like to see me do something lighter, and I actually wouldn't mind doing something lighter. All my characters so far have had dead parents. So maybe it was time for a comedy."

In the film, Campbell stars as Amy Post, the mistress of married billionaire tycoon Charles Newman, played by McDermott. "She's a girl who has a good heart, but doesn't know who to give it to," Neve says of the character. "She also finds herself attracted to unavailable men."

Matthew Perry plays Oscar Novak, an architect vying to design a cultural center being financed by the billionaire. Because Newman believes Novak is gay, he enlists him to keep tabs on Amy, who also assumes Oscar is gay. "And, in this case," Perry says, "he can't correct them. In the process, in his friendship with Neve Campbell, he drops all that guy stuff, like all that trying-to-sleep-with-her stuff, and they actually get to know each other." Predictably, Amy falls in love with Oscar, Oscar falls in love with Amy, and in the end, his mistaken identity is revealed and love blooms for everyone but the billionaire. The critics weren't particularly kind.

But just as Campbell was able to brush off the disappointing reception of 54, *Three to Tango* also seemed to be little more than a temporary setback. Neve barely gave a backward look, having too much to plan for in her future, including expressed desires to expand her career to behind the camera. "If there aren't a lot of female projects out there, then I'll create them. I definitely want to direct one day and I *will* move into directing one day," Campbell states. "But, at the moment, I don't have a whole lot of time."

However, Neve was finding enough time to bring a little romance back in her life. One of her first post-divorce boyfriends had been her *Scream* co-star Matthew Lillard. When asked about their relationship, Lillard was hesitant. "I'm covering really dangerous ground here," he said, choosing just to say that Neve was a "genuinely kind and nurturing" person. Then in April 1999, while filming *Three to Tango*, stories circulated that she and co-star Matthew Perry seemed to be past the just-friends stage when spotted out and about together, but those rumors turned out to be nothing more. However, more accurate were reports that while in Toronto working on *Tango*, Neve became romantically linked with John Cusak, who was in Toronto filming the movie *Pushing Tin*. Later, Neve traveled to the Calgary location of Cusak's next project, *The Jack Bull*. On July 30, 1999, WBAL radio in Baltimore went so far as to broadcast an unsubstantiated report that Campbell and Cusak were engaged.

Cusak proved as private as Campbell, but a lot more testy, calling the media interest in their relationship unhealthy, saying he considered it "absolutely sinister that people need to live vicariously through celebrities. They instantly conclude their own happiness is not as real as a celebrity's. I've been the subject of magazine covers and I've slept with some of the women who've been featured in those magazines. I can tell you those lives have been airbrushed for those articles. I know for certain that when I read one of the articles written about me, I seem so much more interesting than I know I am."

Not too surprisingly, at the time the official party line was that Cusak and Campbell were "just good friends." "People can become

SOFIA COPPOLA / VISAGES

very judgmental and make a lot of assumptions if they know too much about your private life," Campbell explains. "And I just don't want to have to deal with that. There's enough pressure as it is." In the end, the relationship cooled, and Neve and John really are just friends nowadays.

With the end of her *Party of Five* commitment in sight, Neve seemed to enter her final year on the series with a new perspective. After years of fighting feelings of being imprisoned, she suddenly appeared to appreciate some of the constraints being on a series had provided. "As crazy as things might seem now, it could be going a lot faster," she said. "People keep asking me if I wish I didn't have a TV series, because then I would be able to be in more movies, but I think *Party of Five* is a good thing in that way. It's holding me back from doing too much. Having too many movies out at once can be a bad thing. If this is the pace my career is meant to go at, I don't want to question that. If it speeds up or slows down at some point, that's what it was meant to be."

For as far as the eye could see at the moment, there was no letup in sight to Neve's career. In addition to *Scream 3*, she had several other films in the pipeline including *Panic* opposite William H. Macy. *Panic* was written by Henry Bromell, an award-winning writer whose television work includes *I'll Fly Away*, *Northern Exposure*, and *Chicago Hope*. The script was considered one of Hollywood's hot properties, with many actresses hoping to land the hairdresser role that ultimately went to Neve. "Henry Bromell is a fantastic writer," Campbell enthuses, "and he's also the director on this project. It's really nice to be working on this, a project that is not attached to a studio. Everyone is just doing it because they love the script. We're really doing it for the heart and for the creativity of it. I think that is why he was able to get such a great cast. For me, I feel like I am growing a lot just by working with these people."

Another project was *Drowning Mona*, a comedy starring Danny DeVito and Bette Midler. Midler plays Mona Dearly, the most hated woman in the town of Verblanck. When Mona turns up murdered, the entire town of four hundred and sixty people become suspects.

The project closest to Neve's heart, however, is a film tentatively called *Move*. It tells the story of a young girl who comes to New York to become a classical ballet dancer and finds herself in a love — and dance — triangle. "I would love to incorporate my dance into something, be it a film or TV project or go back to the theater," Neve says. She allows that "it's a tough one, though — musicals aren't as popular now as they once were." However, Warner Brothers studio is banking that Neve's popularity will be the catalyst necessary to reinvigorate the genre.

As her future begins to unfold, for Neve it remains, as it always has, about the work. "A little bit of an obsessive-compulsive disorder," Neve says, describing herself. "I become obsessive about the littlest things, like fixing the remote in my hot tub. If I fixate on something I'll spend hours on it. I am that way in my career, as well. I'm lucky enough to have a job that I love — not many people have that. I love that I have enough money not to worry about money, and to be able to help my family and friends." Although she willingly admits it's nice not to worry about her finances, money is not what drew her to acting in the first place. "I've got a lot to love about my life. Don't get me wrong — I like to get paid. But what do you do with anything over $10 million? After that, it doesn't make any sense." More important to Campbell is finding balance in her life and work. "I'm happy with the decisions I've made. I would like to continue trying different things and continue being inspired to challenge myself. I'm young, I've got a lot of time."

April 2000 marked the end of another chapter in Neve's life, saying goodbye to *Party of Five*, the series that opened the door for her. When asked what she'd do with herself when the series was done, Campbell seemed unsure. "I'll probably travel a bit. I want to go to Egypt or Indonesia." But then again, she felt compelled to add, "If something comes along that I really want to do, then I'll do it. But otherwise, I'll just take a break for a while. I'll just relax."

Sure she will.

Neve Filmography

In looking over Neve's body of work through 1999, one thing that stands out is that she is not an actress fearful of dashing anyone's preconceived image of her. Campbell's choices reflect her personal vision, which manages to balance the commercial with the artistic. Not all of her choices work, but even when these films fall short of their potential, there's always something interesting to watch about Neve herself. Her ability to fill the screen is what cinematic charisma is all about.

Catwalk, 1992
(Television Series)

Brief Plot Summary *An hour long drama about six young adults who form a rock band called Catwalk. But their hoped-for road to success — and a record deal — is littered with personal and professional pitfalls.*

Of Special Note Then relative unknown Jamie Walters guest-starred as singer Jeff Kuzak.

Critical Comment "Youth must be misserved."

Production Credits
Directors: Jerry Ciccoritti, Steve DiMarco, Ken Girotti, Eleanor Lindo

Cast	Lisa Butler	Sierra
	Neve Campbell	**Daisy McKenzie (1992)**
	Christopher Lee Clements	Atlas
	Keram Malicki-Sánchez	Johnny Camden
	Paul Popowich	Jesse Carlson
	Kelli Taylor	Mary Owens
	David Fraser	Merlino (1992)
	Polly Shannon	Nina Moore (1992–94)

The Passion of John Ruskin, 1994
(Short Film)

Brief Plot Summary *Nineteenth-century art critic John Ruskin falls in love with a young woman, Effie, who upsets his notion of artistic beauty.*

Of Special Note This film is fourteen minutes long. The real John Ruskin is best known for his 1856 work *Modern Painters III*.

Critical Comment "Sadly, Neve doesn't get nekkid. Damn."

Production Credits

Director: Alex Chapple
Writer: Alex Chapple
Producer: John Gundy

Cast	**Neve Campbell**	**Rose**
	Mark McKinney	John Ruskin

Paint Cans, 1994
(Film)

Brief Plot Summary *A spoof of making a film under the auspices of government sponsorship.*

Of Special Note Financed by the National Film Board of Canada.

Critical Comment "A brilliant satire on the Canadian film industry."

Production Credits

Director: Paul Donovan
Writer: Paul Donovan
Producers: Paul Donovan, Alan MacGillivray, Stephen J. Turnbull

Cast	Chas Lawther	Wick Burns
	Martha Burns	Melda
	Bruce Greenwood	Vittorio Musso
	Andy Jones	Neville Lewis
	Paul Gross	Morton Ridgewell
	Anne-Marie McDonald	Inge Von Nerthus
	Neve Campbell	**Tristesse**
	Kelly-Ruth Mercier	Tamanee
	Jennie Overton	Anna
	Jim Swansburg	Waiter

The Dark, 1994
(Film)

Brief Plot Summary *A horror film in which a doctor searches for a prehistoric rat-like creature whose blood holds the magical power to heal. In order to stay close to a food source, the creature lives in burrows beneath cemeteries. The doctor must contend with an FBI agent out to kill the creature, which ate his partner.*

Tagline "It will consume you."

Of Special Note Brion James, a legend in the B-movie world, played the crazed FBI agent. James, who died on August 7, 1999, was best known for his role in *Blade Runner* as one of the murderous replicants who tells Harrison Ford, "Wake up. Time to die." The six-foot-three actor once noted, "I rarely live through a film. I've been boiled in oil, I've had my head ripped off by a freeway overpass, and I've been thrown off a cliff. . . . I've killed a lot of people, too."

Critical Comment "Dull junk that's only notable for having Neve Campbell (before her turns in the *Scream* movies) in the cast."

Production Credits
Director: Craig Pryce
Writer: Robert Cooper
Producers: Robert Bergman, Craig Pryce

Cast	Stephen McHattie	Hunter
	Scott Wickware	Carl Miller
	Brion James	Buckner
	Desmond Campbell	FBI Agent
	Dennis O'Connor	Jake
	Jaimz Woolvett	Ed
	Cynthia Belliveau	Tracy
	Bruce Beaton	Biker
	Addison Bell	Al the Cook
	Robbie Rox	Biker 2
	Ian MacDonald	Biker 3
	Neve Campbell	**Jesse Donovan**
	Christopher Bondy	Gabe
	William Lynn	Arnold

Web of Deceit, 1994
(Television Movie)

Brief Plot Summary *Spouses Corbin Bernsen and Amanda Pays star in this thriller about a couple whose world is turned upside down when their newborn son disappears, and the mother, who's suffering from postpartum depression, comes under suspicion.*

Of Special Note The alternate title for this MOW was *I Know My Son Is Alive*.

Production Credits
Director: Bill Corcoran
Writers: Joseph Broido, Raymond Hartung
Executive Producers: Les Alexander, Don Enright

Cast	Corbin Bernsen	Mark
	Amanda Pays	Katherine
	Al Waxman	Herb
	Mimi Kuzyk	Laura
	Neve Campbell	**Beth**
	Tom McCamus	Falcone
	Sveta Kohli	Foreign Nanny
	Kim Coates	Detective Griffi
	Albert Schultz	Bernie
	Nigel Bennet	Eisner
	Carlton Watson	Detective Gaffey
	Peter Krantz	Scott
	Caroline Yeager	Bank Teller
	Jeremy Harris	College Kid
	Helen Beavis	Mrs. Lassell

The Forget-Me-Not Murders, 1994
(Television Movie)

Brief Plot Summary *This installment in the Janek series of made-for-television films has the detective tracking a serial killer who leaves a flower with each of his victims. This time, Janek also has a personal motive because one of the victims was his niece.*

Of Special Note Campbell is the serial killer's fourth victim. Helen Shaver, who plays Monique, would later appear in *The Craft* with Neve.

Critical Comment "A pretty good film on its own, with grisly murders, only a few suspects, and a lot of talking. Watch it to see Neve Campbell in her pre-*Party of Five* and *Scream* days."

Production Credits

Director: Robert Iscove

Cast

Richard Crenna	Frank Janek
Tyne Daly	Dr. Archer
Cliff Gorman	Aaron
Philip Bosco	Chief
Diane D'Aquila	Alexis
John Verson	Boyce
Helen Shaver	Monique
Angel David	Leo Titus
Michael Genet	Agent Tapper
Neve Campbell	**Jessica Foy**
Marcia Bennett	Laura Foy
Amber Lea Weston	Fran
Yannick Bisson	Greg Gale
Dean McDermott	Agent Alex
Heidi Hatashita	Agent Kay

Party of Five, 1994–

(Television Series)

Brief Plot Summary *After a drunk driver kills the Salingers, their five children vow to stay together. The series follows their struggles to grow up without the benefit of parents.*

Of Special Note For the first two years of the series, it was constantly threatened with cancelation. But its critical acclaim, as well as the support of then Fox Entertainment president Peter Roth, kept the show on the air long enough for it to find an audience.

Accolades

1996 Golden Globe: Best Dramatic TV Series

1995 Humanitas Award

1997 YoungStar Award: Best Performance by a Young Actress in a Drama (Lacey Chabert)

Critical Comment "How did Fox put such a wonderful show like *Party of Five* on its schedule? Are they doing penance for all the junk? Since when do they do socially responsible programming, putting on a show with conscience?"

Production Credits
Directors: Various
Executive Producers: Christopher Keyser, Amy Lippman

Regular Cast

Scott Wolf	Bailey Salinger
Matthew Fox	Charlie Salinger
Neve Campbell	**Julia Salinger Holbrook (1994–2000)**
Lacey Chabert	Claudia Salinger
Paula Devicq	Kirsten Bennett Thomas Salinger (1994–1996, 1997–)
Jeremy London	Griffin Holbrook (1995–)
Jennifer Love Hewitt	Sarah Reeves (1995–1999)
Alexondra Lee	Callie Martel (1996–1997)
Michael A. Goorjian	Justin Thompson (1995–1996)
Scott Grimes	Will McCorkle
Mitchell Anderson	Ross Werkman (1994–)
Jennifer Aspen	Daphne Jablonsky (1998–)
Scott Bairstow	Ned Grayson (1998–1999)
Ben Browder	Sam Brody (1996–1997)
Andrew Cavarno	Owen Salinger (1995–1998)
Steven Cavarno	Owen Salinger (1995–1998)
Wilson Cruz	Victor (1999–)
Tim Dekay	Paul Thomas (Kirsten's ex-husband) (1997–)
Dan Lauria	Coach Russ Petrocelli (1996–1997)
Jessica Lundy	Nina DiMayo (1997)
Tom Mason	Joe Mangus (1994–)
Heather McComb	Maggie (1998–)
Kathleen Noone	Ellie Bennett
Carroll O'Connor	Jacob Gordon (1996)
Brandon Porter	Owen Salinger
Taylor Porter	Owen Salinger
Harold Pruett	Cooper (1996)
Nicholas Pryor	Gene Bennett

Adam Scott	Josh Macon (1998–)
Cari Shayne	Nina DiMayo (1994–1995)
Jacob Smith	Owen Salinger (1998–)
Tamara Taylor	Grace Wilcox (1996–1997)
Paige Turco	Annie Mott (1997–1998)
Megan Ward	Jill Holbrook (1994–1995)
Brenda Wehle	Dr. Rabin (1997–1998)

Baree, 1994

(Television Movie)

Brief Plot Summary *A movie about a dog.*

Of Special Note *Baree* was based on the book *Baree, Son of Kazan*. Two previous films were also produced, in 1918 and 1925.

Production Credits

Director: Arnaud Sélignac

Writer: Jonathan Hales; James Oliver Curwood, on whose book the movie was based

Executive Producer: Robert Réa

Cast		
	Jeff Fahey	Paul
	Jacques Weber	Pierre
	Lorne Brass	Taggart
	Neve Campbell	**Nepeese**
	Geneviève Rochette	Marie
	Billy Two Rivers	Broken Foot

Love Child, 1995

(Short Film)

Production Credits

Director: Patrick Sisam

Cast		
	Neve Campbell	**Deidre**

The Witching Hour, 1996

(Documentary)

Brief Plot Summary *A behind-the-scenes look at the making of the film* The Craft.

Of Special Note The documentary incorporated a veritable witchfest of other films, including *The Wizard of Oz*, *Carrie*, *Damien: Omen II*, and *The Witches of Eastwick*.

Production Credits

Director: Reba Merrill

Writer: Paul Wiesepape

Executive Producer: Reba Merrill

Cast		
	Fairuza Balk	Herself
	Robin Tunney	Herself
	Neve Campbell	**Herself**
	Pat Devin	Herself

The Canterville Ghost, 1996

(Television Movie)

Brief Plot Summary *When an American teenager, Ginny, moves into Canterville Hall in England with her family, things start going bump in the night. Eventually, Ginny meets the hall's resident ghost, Sir Simon de Canterville, who enlists her aid to help free him from his curse.*

Of Special Note This Oscar Wilde short story has been made into three feature films and three TV movies. Simon de Canterville was played by Charles Laughton in the 1944 film version, which also starred Margaret O'Brien as Ginny. On TV, Sir John Gielgud has embodied the courtly spirit.

Accolades

1996 Emmy: Oustanding Individual Achievement in Music Composition for a Miniseries or a Special (Ernest Troost)

1996 Family Film Awards: Best Actor (Patrick Stewart); Best Actress (Neve Campbell); Outstanding Television Film

Critical Comment "Stewart's Sir Simon is a tragic figure of considerable stateliness and poignancy. But he is very seldom funny. . . . Campbell is appealing in her own right, and (director) MacCartney further advances her cause by allotting the young actress even more moist-eyed close-ups than the little O'Brien lass got back in '44."

Production Credits
Director: Sydney MacCartney
Writer: Robert Benedetti; from a story by Oscar Wilde
Executive Producers: Robert Benedetti, Richard Welsh

Cast		
	Patrick Stewart	Sir Simon de Canterville
	Neve Campbell	**Ginny Otis**
	Joan Sims	Mrs. Umney
	Donald Sinden	Mr. Umney
	Cherie Lunghi	Lucille Otis
	Edward Wiley	Hiram Otis
	Leslie Phillips	George, Lord Canterville
	Daniel Betts	Francis, Duke of Cheshire
	Ciarán Fitzgerald	Adam Otis
	Raymond Pickard	Washington Otis

The Craft, 1996
(Film)

Brief Plot Summary *When a new girl moves to town, she hooks up with three other high-school misfits. They begin to dabble in witchcraft, unleashing a formidable power. At first, they use their powers in almost childish pranks, but their spells eventually get out of hand, pitting the girls against one another.*

Tagline "Welcome to the witching hour."

Accolades
1998 MTV Movie Award: Best Fight (knife fight between Fairuza Balk and Robin Tunney)

Critical Comment "The film loses its humor when it pours on ho-hum horror effects (heavy on serpents) in a showdown between Balk, empowered into a full-blown punk Medusa frenzy, and Tunney, who wants to stop the insanity. If only *The Craft* were as fresh as its enchanting lead quartet."

Production Credits

Director: Andrew Fleming

Writers: Peter Filardi, Andrew Fleming; story by Peter Filardi

Executive Producer: Ginny Nugent

Cast

Fairuza Balk	Nancy Downs
Robin Tunney	Sarah Bailey
Neve Campbell	**Bonnie**
Rachel True	Rochelle
Christine Taylor	Laura Lizzie
Skeet Ulrich	Chris
Assumpta Serna	Lirio
Cliff De Young	Mr. Bailey
Breckin Meyer	Mitt
Nathaniel Marston	Trey
Helen Shaver	Grace
Jeanine Jackson	Jenny
Brenda Strong	Doctor
Elizabeth Guber	Laura's Friend
Jennifer Greenhut	Laura's Friend
Arthur Senzy	Vagrant
Endre Hules	Monsieur Thepet
Mark Conlon	Swimming Coach
Christine Louise Berry	Stewardess
William Newman	Street Preacher
Erin Tavin	Homeless Mother
Rod Britt	Priest
Brogan Roche	Insurance Man
Rebecca McLaughlin	Biology Teacher
Tony Genaro	Bus Driver
Janet Rotblatt	Homeroom Teacher
Jason Filardi	Paramedic
Karyn J. Dean	Whispering Girl
Danielle Koenig	Whispering Girl
Janet Eilber	Sarah's Mother
Esther Scott	Nurse

Scream, 1996
(Film)

Brief Plot Summary *A serial killer is stalking Woodboro, murdering teens. In response, students at the local high school begin dressing up as the killer and living out their own horror film. Caught in the middle is Sidney, whose own mother was brutally killed a year earlier and who unknowingly is at the center of the killings.*

Tagline "Make your last breath count."

Of Special Note Bonnie Pointer, Wes Craven, Linda Blair, and Henry Winkler all have uncredited cameos.

Accolades

1998 ASCAP Award: Top Box Office Films
1997 Saturn Award (Academy of Science Fiction, Horror and Fantasy Films): Best Actress (Neve Campbell); Best Writer (Kevin Williamson); and Best Picture
1997 MTV Movie Awards: Best Movie

Critical Comments "What did I think about this movie? As a film critic, I liked it. I liked the in-jokes and the self-aware characters. At the same time, I was aware of the incredible level of gore in this film. It is *really* violent. Is the violence defused by the ironic way the film uses it and comments on it? For me, it was. For some viewers, it will not be, and they will be horrified." *Roger Ebert*

". . . while *Scream* has its frights, it feels more like one of those solve-the-mystery jigsaw puzzles than a real movie. And the too-clever-for-its-own-good ending is a blood-splattered reminder that sometimes parody comes awfully close to what it is mocking." *Susan Wloszczyna, USA Today*

Production Credits

Director: Wes Craven
Writer: Kevin Williamson
Executive Producers: Marianne Maddalena, Bob Weinstein, Harvey Weinstein

Cast

David Arquette	Deputy Dwight "Dewey" Riley
Neve Campbell	**Sidney Prescott**
Courteney Cox	Gale Weathers
Jamie Kennedy	Randy Meeks
Matthew Lillard	Stuart Macher
Rose McGowan	Tatum Riley

Skeet Ulrich	Billy Loomis
Drew Barrymore	Casey Becker
Liev Schreiber	Cotton Weary
W. Earl Brown	Kenny, the Cameraman
Joseph Whipp	Sheriff Burke
Roger L. Jackson	Phone Voice
Kevin Patrick Walls	Steven Orth
David Booth	Casey's Father
Carla Hatley	Casey's Mother
Lawrence Hecht	Neil Prescott
Lois Saunders	Mrs. Tate
Lisa Beach	TV Reporter #1
Tony Kilbert	TV Reporter #2
C.W. Morgan	Hank Loomis
Lee McCain	Mrs. Riley
Troy Bishop	Expelled Teen #1
Ryan Kennedy	Expelled Teen #2
Leonora Scelfo	Cheerleader in Bathroom
Nancy Ann Ridder	Girl in Bathroom
Lisa Canning	Reporter with Mask
Bonnie Wood	Young Girl in Video Store

Scream 2, 1997
(Film)

Brief Plot Summary *Sometime after the events of* Scream, *when it was discovered that two killers had been slaughtering half the town's population, a movie about the killings has been made, called* Stab. *The local college students flock to the movie, donning masks like those of the killer and scaring one another. But what they don't realize is that there is now another killer among them.*

Tagline "Someone has taken their love of sequels one step too far."

Accolades

1998 ASCAP Award: Top Box Office Films

1998 Blockbuster Entertainment Award: Favorite Actor, Horror (David Arquette); Favorite Actress, Horror (Neve Campbell); Favorite Supporting Actor, Horror (Jamie Kennedy)

1998 MTV Movie Award: Best Female Performance (Neve Campbell)

Critical Comment "After a while, the scariness of bodies bloodily dispatched tops out, but the jokes keep on coming, as do the ain't-it-cool pop-cultural references and inside-showbiz details. (Just the casting of Tori Spelling, Laurie Metcalf, and David Warner scores points right there.)"

Production Credits

Director: Wes Craven

Writer: Kevin Williamson

Executive Producers: Bob Weinstein, Harvey Weinstein, Kevin Williamson

Cast		
	David Arquette	Deputy Dwight "Dewey" Riley
	Neve Campbell	**Sidney Prescott**
	Courteney Cox	Gale Weathers
	Sarah Michelle Gellar	Casey "CiCi" Cooper
	Jamie Kennedy	Randy Meeks
	Duane Martin	Joel, the Cameraman
	Laurie Metcalf	Reporter Debbie Salt
	Elise Neal	Hallie
	Jerry O'Connell	Derek
	Timothy Olyphant	Mickey
	Jada Pinkett	Maureen Evans
	Liev Schreiber	Cotton Weary
	Lewis Arquette	Chief Louis Hartley
	Rebecca Gayheart	Sorority Sister Lois
	Portia de Rossi	Sorority Sister Murphy
	Omar Epps	Phil Stevens
	Tori Spelling	Herself/Sidney Prescott in *Stab*
	Heather Graham	Casey in *Stab*
	Paulette Patterson	Usher Giving Out Costumes
	Rasila Schroeder	Screaming Girl in Aisle
	Roger L. Jackson	Phone Voice
	Peter Deming	Popcorn Boy
	Molly Gross	Theater Girl #1
	Rebecca McFarland	Theater Girl #2
	Kevin Williamson	Cotton's Interviewer
	Sandy Heddings	Girl in Dorm Hallway
	Dave Allen Clark	Reporter Outside Theater
	Joe Washington	Reporter #1
	Angie Dillard	Reporter #2
	John Patrick	Reporter #3
	Craig Shoemaker	Film Teacher
	Joshua Jackson	Film Class Guy #1
	Walter Franks	Film Class Guy #2

Nina Petronzio	Film Class Mopey Girl
Stephanie Belt	Reporter #4
Richard Bruce Doughty	Reporter #5
Marisol Nichols	Dawnie
Cornelia Kiss	Coroner at CiCi's House
Lucy Lin	ER Doctor
Philip Pavel	Officer Andrews
Tim Hillman	Captain F. Down
Nancy O'Dell	Tori's Interviewer
Luke Wilson	Billy in *Stab*
David Warner	Drama Teacher Gus Gold

Lion King II: Simba's Pride, 1998

(Made for Video)

Brief Plot Summary *More family feuding in the jungle. Simba and Nala's daughter, Kiara, sneaks out on her babysitters — Timon and Pumba — and while in the forbidden lands befriends Kovu. What she doesn't know is that Kovu's mother, Zira, was Scar's mate and has planned for Kovu to overthrow Simba and become king.*

Of Special Note Neve's *Party of Five* castmate, Lacey Chabert, has a small role.

Critical Comment "Hewing to the exotic epic look of the original blockbuster, the new direct-to-video sequel *The Lion King II: Simba's Pride* is enchanting small-screen entertainment that feels big."

Production Credits

Directors: Darrell Rooney, Rob LaDuca
Primary Writers: Flip Kobler, Cindy Marcus
Producer: Jeannine Roussel

Voice Cast

Matthew Broderick	Simba
Neve Campbell	**Adult Kiara**
Andy Dick	Nuka
Robert Guillaume	Rafiki
James Earl Jones	Mufasa
Moira Kelly	Nala
Nathan Lane	Timon
Jason Marsden	Adult Kovu
Suzanne Pleshette	Zira

Ernie Sabella	Pumba
Liz Callaway	Adult Kiara
Lacey Chabert	Young Vitani
Cam Clarke	Simba
Ashley Edner	Young Kiara
Edward Hibbert	Zazu
Michelle Horn	Young Kiara
Jennifer Lien	Adult Vitani
Crysta Macalush	Young Vitani
Gene Miller	Adult Kovu
Ryan O'Donohue	Young Kovu
Charity Sanoy	Young Kiara

Hairshirt, 1998
(Film)

Brief Plot Summary *After being rejected by her boyfriend, a young woman tries to sabotage his subsequent relationship.*

Of Special Note This film, which premiered at the Toronto International Film Festival, was produced by Neve and her brother Christian.

Critical Comments "There is no other way to say it so I'll be blunt. Neve Campbell is annoying."

"Neve Campbell isn't an actress anymore. She's a bona fide movie star. Which is why she's well suited for the role of the narcissistic Hollywood starlet Renee Weber in Dean Paras' directorial debut, *Hairshirt*. The egotistical Weber sure isn't a stretch."

Production Credits
Director: Dean Paras
Writer: Dean Paras; story by Nate Tuck and Katie Wright
Executive Producers: Christian Campbell, Neve Campbell, Dean Paras

Cast

Dean Paras	Danny Reilly
Katie Wright	Corey Wells
Neve Campbell	**Renee Weber**
Kimberly Huie	Kimberly
Stefan Brogren	Tim
David DeLuise	Peter Angelo
Rebecca Gayheart	Jennifer

Wild Things, 1998
(Film)

Brief Plot Summary *A high-school teacher is accused of raping one of his students, whose mother is not only rich and connected but also the teacher's former lover. A complicated game of intrigue and double-cross results that isn't fully resolved until the end credits.*

Tagline "They can turn you on or turn on you."

Accolades

1999 Blockbuster Favorite Supporting Actress: Suspense (Daphne Rubin-Vega)

1998 Los Angeles Film Critics Association: Best Supporting Actor (Bill Murray) (also for his performance in *Rushmore*).

Critical Comment "In this exhilaratingly campy, intricately constructed comic film noir, all the things that seemed to simmer under Campbell's nervous smile in *Scream* burst to the surface. With shaggy, cherry-red hair, eggplant-colored lipstick and tattoos snaking down her knuckles, Campbell is outrageously good as basket case Suzie Toller." *Michelle Goldberg, Salon*

Production Credits

Director: John McNaughton
Writer: Stephen Peters
Executive Producer: Kevin Bacon

Cast		
	Kevin Bacon	Ray Duquette
	Matt Dillon	Sam Lombardo
	Neve Campbell	**Suzie Toller**
	Theresa Russell	Sandra Van Ryan
	Denise Richards	Kelly Van Ryan
	Daphne Rubin-Vega	Gloria Perez
	Robert Wagner	Tom Baxter
	Bill Murray	Ken Bowden
	Carrie Snodgress	Ruby
	Jeff Perry	Bryce Hunter
	Cory Pendergast	Jimmy Leach
	Marc Macaulay	Walter
	Toi Svane	Nicole
	Dennis Neal	Art Maddox
	Diane Adams	School Secretary

Paulo Benedeti	Kirk
Eduardo Yáñez	Frankie Condo
Jennifer Bini Taylor	Barbara Baxter
Victoria Bass	Judge
Ted Bartsch	Bailiff
Leonor Anthony	Ken's Secretary
Antoni Corone	Police Chief

54, 1998
(Film)

Brief Plot Summary *Welcome now, my friends, to the show that never ends . . . a kid from New Jersey crosses the bridge and ends up working at Studio 54. Eventually he comes to see all the glitz, glamour, and drugs for what they are — glitz, glamour, and drugs.*

Tagline "Welcome to the Party"

Accolades

1998 Razzie: Worst Actor (Ryan Phillippe); Worst Supporting Actress (Ellen Albertini Dow)

Critical Comment "The film tries to toss *Saturday Night Fever*'s bridge-and-tunnel dreamers into the '70s' hottest disco. But for that to work, you need verve, edge, and Travolta. All those are absent here." *Susan Wloszczyna, USA Today*

Production Credits

Director: Mark Christopher

Writer: Mark Christopher

Executive Producers: Don Carmody, Bobby Cohen, Bob Weinstein, Harvey Weinstein

Cast		
	Ryan Phillippe	Shane O'Shea
	Salma Hayek	Anita
	Sela Ward	Billie Auster
	Breckin Meyer	Greg Randazzo
	Sherry Stringfield	Viv
	Neve Campbell	**Julie Black**
	Mike Myers	Steve Rubell
	Heather Matarazzo	Grace O'Shea
	Ellen Albertini Dow	Disco Dottie

Mark Ruffalo	Richie
Jay Goede	Buck
Lorri Bagley	Patti
Cameron Mathison	Atlanta
Noam Jenkins	Romeo
Patrick Taylor	Tarzan
Aemilia Robinson	Kelly O'Shea
Daniel Lapaine	Doorman
Thelma Houston	Herself
Mary Griffin	Disco Star
Don Carrier	Julian
Robert Bauer	Roland
Bruno Miguel	Boyd
Laura Catalano	Rochelle
Kohl Sudduth	Brett
Lauren Hutton	Liz Vangelder
James Binkley	Rubell's Bodyguard
Arthur J. Nascarella	IRS Agent
John Himes	IRS Agent
Vieslav Krystyan	Photographer
Barbara Radecki	TV Host
Ron Jeremy	Ron
Sean Gregory Sullivan	Andy Warhol
David Blacker	Bouncer
Niki Holt	Alpine Inn Waitress
Bruce MacVittie	Music Producer
Kabriel Lilly	Little Girl
Louis Negin	Truman Capote
Michael York	Ambassador
Elio Fiorucci	Himself
Lina Felice	Nicaraguan Woman
Drake Thoren	Man on Horseback
Emmanuel Mark	Talent Manager
Erika Alexander	Ciel
Peter Bogdanovich	Elaine's Patron
Victor Browne	VIP Patron
Cindy Crawford	VIP Patron
Sheryl Crow	VIP Patron
Vincent de Paul	Disco Kid Outside
Art Garfunkel	Elaine's Patron
Beverly Johnson	Elaine's Patron

Lorna Luft	Elaine's Patron
Coati Mundi	DJ
Valerie Perrine	Elaine's Patron
Donald Trump	VIP Patron
Frederique Van Der Wal	VIP Patron
Veronica Webb	VIP Patron

Panic, 1999
(Film)

Brief Plot Summary *A young man, trying to assert himself with his controlling family, meets and falls in love with a passionate woman in between therapy sessions.*

Production Credits
Director: Henry Bromwell
Writer: Henry Bromwell
Executive Producer: David Cooper

Cast		
	Neve Campbell	**Sarah**
	John Ritter	Josh
	David Dorfman	Sammy
	William H. Macy	Alex
	Erica Ortega	Rachel
	Miguel Sandoval	Larson
	Donald Sutherland	Michael
	Nicholle Tom	Tracy

Move, 1999
(Film)

Brief Plot Summary *A young woman moves to New York to pursue her dream of being a professional dancer and falls in love with two very different men.*

Production Credits
Writer: Eric Guggenheim
Producers: Neve Campbell, Arlene Forster, Eric Guggenheim, Tony Ludwig, Ben Myron, Alan Riche

Cast **Neve Campbell**

Three to Tango, 1999
(Film)

Brief Plot Summary *A rich guy asks an associate he assumes is gay to keep an eye on his girlfriend. Wouldn't you know it? The gay guy isn't, and he falls in love with the rich guy's girl, who also happens to think he's gay.*

Tagline "All's fair in the war of love."

Production Credits

Director: Damon Santostefano

Writers: Rodney Patrick Vaccaro, Aline Brosh McKenna; story by Rodney Patrick Vaccaro

Executive Producers: Lawrence Abramson, Bruce Berman

Cast		
	Matthew Perry	Oscar Novak
	Neve Campbell	**Amy Post**
	Dylan McDermott	Charles Newman
	Bob Balaban	Strauss
	Oliver Platt	Peter Steinberg

Scream 3, 2000
(Film)

Brief Plot Summary *Hoping to put her harrowing encounters with killers behind her, Sidney Prescott moves to Hollywood to be an actress. As movie luck would have it, she gets cast in* Stab 3, *the film franchise based on the real-life killings back in Woodboro. Before long, the killings begin again. . . .*

Tagline "In order for Sidney Prescott to survive the future she must look to the past."

Production Credits

Director: Wes Craven

Writer: Ehren Kruger

Producers: Cathy Konrad, Marianne Maddalena, Kevin Williamson

Cast		
	David Arquette	Deputy Dwight "Dewey" Riley
	Neve Campbell	**Sidney Prescott**
	Courteney Cox	Gale Weathers
	Patrick Dempsey	Buddy Laflour
	Carrie Fisher	Holly Westchester
	Scott Foley	Roman Banks

Lance Henriksen	Detective Corruthers
Kate Hudson	Melanie Watson
Roger L. Jackson	Phone Voice
Matthew Keeslar	Tom Prinze
Jenny McCarthy	Sarah Darling
Emily Mortimer	Helen Johanson
Parker Posey	Natalie O'Dell/Gale in *Stab 3*
Deon Richmond	Gabe/Joel in *Stab 3*

Drowning Mona, 2000
(Film)

Brief Plot Summary *Someone has killed Mona, and half the people in the small town where she lived, Verblank, become suspects. Oh, yeah — it's a comedy.*

Tagline "1 Murder. 460 Prime Suspects." "Not so much of a *who done it?* as a *who didn't?*"

Production Credits
Director: Nick Gomez
Writer: Peter Steinfeld
Executive Producers: Danny DeVito, Michael Shamberg, Stacey Sher, Jonathan Weisgal

Cast

Casey Affleck	Bobby Calzone
Neve Campbell	**Ellen**
Jamie Lee Curtis	Rona, the Waitress
Danny DeVito	Wyatt Rash
Yul Vazquez	Frenchy
William Fichtner	Phil Dearly
Bette Midler	Mona Dearly
Marcus Thomas	Jeff Dearly

Works Cited

(In addition to the reference materials listed below, the author has also made extensive use of press-related film and television production materials and press-related interviews.)

"Any Witch Way She Can." *Australian TV Hits*. Aug. 1996.

Applebaum, Stephen. "Scare Stories: Wes Craven Interview." *Independent*. Apr. 25, 1998.

Ascher-Walsh, Rebecca. "The Worst Years of Our Lives." *Entertainment Weekly*. Jan. 16, 1998.

Australian TV Week. Sept. 20, 1997.

Banks, Samantha, Brandon Coburn, and Michelle Erland. "Kidsday: Talking With Lacey Chabert." *Newsday*. Mar. 8, 1995.

Bryson, Jodi. "Neve Campbell." *Sassy*. June 1996.

"Campbell's Coup." *TV Guide*. Aug. 14, 1996.

Cooney, Jenny. "Cursed!" *Australian TV Week*. June 15, 1996.

Crook, John. *TV Data* Entertainment Features Syndicate.

Cunneff, Tom, and Susan SchindeHette. "Couples: Who'll Be the Boss?" *People*. Mar. 28, 1994.

Dunn, Jancee. "Why Neve Can Finally Smile." *Cosmopolitan*. Oct. 1999.

Ebert, Roger. Review of *The Craft*. *Chicago Sun-Times*. 1996.

Empire. Jan. 1999.

Entertainment Tonight. Interview.

Farley, Christopher John. "The Call of the Wild: Sex, Death, Betrayal." *Time* (international edition). Mar. 23, 1998.

——. "Wild Thing Neve Campbell Sizzles in a New Movie and Gets Ready for a Jump to Full-Time movie stardom." *Time* (international edition). Mar. 30, 1998.

Fay, Jeanne. "Neve on the Edge." *Buzz Magazine*. Jan. 1998.

Fretts, Bruce. "Scare Packages." *Entertainment Weekly*. June 27, 1997.
Goodman, Mark, and Tina Johnson. "Twins Peaking." *People*. Oct. 11, 1993.
Graham, Jeff. *TV Guide*. Sept. 1994.
Graham, Jefferson. "A Family You Should Get to Know." *USA Today*. Nov. 2, 1994.
Guerra, Joey. "Non-90210 Role Lets Tori Spelling Prove Self." *Arizona Republic*. Sept. 9, 1999.
Hensley, Dennis. "Tori Spelling." *Cosmopolitan*. Nov. 1997.
"Hi, It's Neve Calling." *Australian TV Hits*. May 1997.
Hiltbrand, David. "Picks & Pans." *People*. Nov. 2, 1992.
Hobson, Louis B. "Saving David Arquette." *London Free Press*. Apr. 10, 1999.
——. "Campbell Has Had a Wild Life." *London Free Press*. Mar. 18, 1998.
——. "Wolf Feeding on Film Roles." *Calgary Sun*. Apr. 7, 1999.
Hochman, David. "Scream and Scream Again." *Entertainment Weekly*. Nov. 28, 1997.
Hunt, Dennis. "At 100 Episodes, *Party* Still Lively." *USA Today*. Nov. 11, 1998.
Jobling, Kate. "Neve Campbell." *Australian Dolly*. July 1996.
Karger, Dave. "Women on the Verge." *Entertainment Weekly*. June 1996.
Kelleher, Terry. "Stewart Gets Into the Spirit of Things." *People*. Jan. 21, 1996.
Kitman, Marvin. "They're Home Alone." *Newsday*. Sept. 8, 1994.
Krantz, Michael. "The Bard of Gen-Y Hot-Wired Into Today's Teens: Kevin Williamson Is Giving Hollywood Something to Scream About." *Time*. Dec. 15, 1997.
Kronke, David. "*Five* and *2*: It Adds Up." *Los Angeles Times*. Dec. 7, 1997.
Lombardi, Lisa. "*Party of Five*'s Jeremy London on Being Dumped and Waiting for Love." *Twist*. Oct.–Nov. 1997.
"Love Was Actor's *Scream* Come True." Scripps Howard News Service. *Dallas Morning News*. Apr. 19, 1999.
Malcom, Shawna. "*Party* Guest: Olivia d'Abo — Neve Campbell's New Squeeze on *Party of Five*." *Entertainment Weekly*. Apr. 30, 1999.
Mendoza, N.F. "It's Charlie's Choice: To Wed or Not? A Character at the Crossroads." *Newsday*. Dec. 13, 1995.
Mixon, Veronica. "Neve Campbell." *Rough Cut*. Mar. 18–24, 1998.
Modderno, Craig. *Listen Up*.
Moore, Roger. "Bad, Bad Girl." *Journal Now*. Mar. 20, 1998.
Murphy, Mary. "Here's Lacey." *TV Guide*. Aug. 31, 1996.

Murray, Steve. "Review of *Scream 2*." *Atlanta Journal and Constitution*. Dec. 12, 1997.
Nance, Jack, *E! Online*. Dec. 1997.
"Neve and Lacey *Party* On!" *Australian TV Week*. June 7, 1997.
"The New Jamie Lee: Neve Campbell." *Entertainment Weekly*. June 1997.
"Party of One." *Genre*. May 1996.
Pinsker, Beth. "Filmmaker Has a Craven for Himself." *Dallas Morning News*. Dec. 20, 1996.
Portman, Jamie. "An Oasis Amid Chaos: Neve Campbell Is More Than a Horror Actor." *Ottawa Citizen*. Dec. 11, 1997.
Raso, Anne M. "Neve's Witching Hour." *Australian Star*. Nov. 1996.
"The Reigning Canadian." *Australian Who*. July 15, 1996.
Richardson, Anna. *The Big Show*. Nov. 22, 1998.
Richter Campbell, Geri. "Tantrums on the Set, Sex Scenes With Women, Painful Bunion Surgery, and Now an Interview With Mysterious 'Cousin' Geri Richter Campbell: Where Will the Drama End?" *Jane*. May 1999.
Rottenberg, Josh. "Neve Screams Again." *Australian TV Week*. Sept. 20, 1997.
Roush, Matt. "Let the Good Times Roll: *Party of Five* Expects to Entertain a Bigger Crowd." *USA Today*. Aug. 21, 1996.
Schaefer, Stephen. "Arquette's Glad to be Goofy." *USA Today*. Apr. 14, 1999.
SchindeHette, Susan. "Couples: Who'll Be the Boss?" *People*. May 1996.
Schulgasser, Barbara. "Wild Tale of Lust and Deception." *San Francisco Examiner*. Mar. 20, 1998.
Sheh, Stephanie. "Perennial Good Girl Neve Campbell Turns Bad in *Wild Things*." *University Wire*. Mar. 19, 1998.
Slewinski, Christy. "Neve Campbell Strays From the *Party* Line." *New York Daily News*. Aug. 30, 1996.
Snierson, Dan. "Sibling Revelry, Alcoholic Interventions, Loving and Losing: It's All in a Week's Work for TV's Favorite Calamity Clan." *Entertainment Weekly*. Dec. 26, 1997.
Steine, Ruthe. "Wild Sex, Ho-hum Plot." *San Francisco Chronicle*. Mar. 20, 1998.
Strickler, Jeff. "Horror Master Transformed: Craven Appears as Humanities Prof." *Minneapolis Star Tribune*. Dec. 22, 1996.
Susman, Gary. "Skeet Shooting." *Rough Cut*. Dec. 20, 1996.
Svetkey, Benjamin. "Interview With a Vamp." *Entertainment Weekly*. Apr. 10, 1998.

Thomas, Kevin. "Was Craven Spoofs Teen Horror." *Newsday*. Dec. 20, 1996.

Thompson, Bob. "L.A. Life a Scream for Neve." *Toronto Sun*. Dec. 1996.

——. "Christian Campbell Madness: Neve's Big Brother Juggles Acting, Producing and His Hit Musical." *Toronto Sun*. Oct. 25, 1999.

Thompson, Malissa. "Jeremy London." *Seventeen*. Feb. 1996.

Tucker, Ken. "Orphan Hootenanny." *Entertainment Weekly*. Sept. 9. 1994.

Time Out New York. Apr. 29, 1999.

Vanstone, Ellen. "Simply Stunning." *TV Guide* (Canadian edition). Aug. 17, 1996.

Vejnoska, Jill. "The Real Leading Lady of *Scream 2*." *Atlanta Journal and Constitution*. Dec. 16, 1997.

Weeks, Janet. "Young Actresses Take a Walk on the *Wild* Side: Denise Richards Falls for Seductress Role." *USA Today*. Mar. 20, 1998.

Weiner, Sherry. *UniverCity*. Dec. 1997.

Weintraub, Bernard. "Neve Campbell: Red Hot Right Now." *Cosmopolitan*. Jan. 1997.

——. *New York Times*. Mar. 1, 1997.

Wolf, Jeanne. "Skeet's Love Talk." *YM Magazine*. July 1998.

Wollman Rusoff, Jane. "Neve Campbell: Dancing Queen." *Mr. Showbiz*. Jan. 5, 1999.

——. "New Men for Julia Roberts, Neve Campbell." *Mr. Showbiz*. Dec. 12 1997.